F@*K MY LIFE

F.M.L.

FORGIVE ME LORD

EDWARD BOWERS

I have changed some of the names or used nicknames for some of the individuals, in order to preserve their anonymity. The goal in all cases was to protect people's privacy without damaging the integrity of their story.

For information contact

Edward Bowers

eddieabowers@gmail.com

Front Cover Image by Sydney Bowers

Book and Cover design by Eddie Bowers

ISBN: 978-1-67810-531-0

First Edition: February 2020

10 9 8 7 6 5 4 3 2 1

TO

*MY LORD AND SAVIOR JESUS CHRIST, MY THREE
AMAZING CHILDREN, THE PEOPLE THAT HAVE
WATCHED ME GO THROUGH ALL THE UPS AND
DOWNS IN LIFE.*

*TO THE PEOPLE, I HAVE HURT BY MY ACTIONS,
EMOTIONAL OUTBURSTS, AND MY LACK OF
ATTENTION TO YOU AND YOUR NEEDS.*

*TO THE HURT, LOST, BROKEN-HEARTED, AND
CONFUSED.*

*TO THOSE GOING THROUGH STRUGGLES, BROKEN
HOMES, BROKEN MARRIAGES.*

Edward Bowers

Contents

Foreword

It was the apostle Paul who first suggested the idea that the very hardest parts of being us – or what he calls "thorns in the flesh" – have the unexpected potential to become our allies. It is through our thorns, Paul wrote, that the power and grace of God are most vividly manifested in our lives. In his book FML, Eddie shares his personal story of struggle and growth. In a day and age when it isn't common for men to open up and be vulnerable and share their deepest pain and struggles with life, Eddie takes you on an authentic journey that will capture your heart, while inspiring you to face your own "thorns".

By sharing his own struggles and victories, by taking the reader down the road he has traveled and into the deep pain he has experienced and the price he paid, Eddie has done a great job of showing us how God can repurpose potentially destructive "thorns" for good, including anger, fear, sadness, guilt, and negative self-talk so that we can become the best versions of ourselves. And that out of the ashes of hurt and pain can rise up strong men who represent Christ and His love to the world.

Our personal, mental, spiritual, and emotional health depends on this kind of knowledge – and the health and common good of our society require that we examine our own inner landscape. By gaining insight into our broken inner lives, we grow in empathy and love for others. When God initiates healing and growth it isn't just for us, but also for others. His purpose in blessing us is that we might be a blessing to others.

FML will convict you to stand stronger, inspire you to do your own personal growth work and show you that indeed there is hope for today.

Grab this book and get ready to be inspired!

Amy Hill, MA, LPC, CCLC
Building Powerful Marriages for Christian Men
The Powerful Marriage
Warrior Husbands for Christ

Prologue

I thought I had everything just the way I wanted it. Wife, kids, house, friends, job. Things were going to be fine. I had dreams, goals, and aspirations. I just had to stick to the plan, and we would be fine.

I thought I was a good person and had my shit together. Sure, I had made mistakes, who hasn't? But I knew better this time, and I would not do things wrong this time. I had Jesus in my life, and He would protect me, this time it was blessed by God so nothing could go wrong. The past was just that, the past. Life has a funny way of showing you that you need to make changes though. You have your plans, then life happens.

I thought life was supposed to go a little something like this. You are born, you go to school, go to college, get a job. Find the woman you are going to be with the rest of your life, have kids, a dog, a house. Grow old, retire, then die. Family vacations, holidays with family, seems easy and fun, right?

Man, I had no clue. No clue what my life was going to look like, no clue what was going to happen in my life, and no clue it would look nothing like what I just listed above. Maybe I was sheltered, maybe I lied to myself too much, maybe I allowed people to influence me too much. Maybe I was just born different from other people.

Maybe I was born a monster so to speak. I don't really know. What I do know is that people go through shit in life and that shit can either make you or break you or worse yet, break other people.

Throughout life, my highs were the highest, and my lows were the lowest. The transitions from the highs to the lows were fast, like in the blink of an eye. I would have everything, then it was all gone. Now the same did not stand for the transitions from the lows to the highs. I always seemed to have to work double-time to get back up. The climbs back up, however, seemed to create just as must devastation for others as the falls.

Then add to all of that, mental health issues. As a person who now deals with depression and anxiety, with maybe a dash of PTSD, everything becomes a whirlwind of disaster that is harder and harder to deal with. But with all that I push forward, and just dig deep so that I can maybe change my old ways so that I can live a happy life.

I remember the day she left me like it was yesterday. The pain in my gut. I remember praying over, and over again for God to speak to me, change me, help me. I remember the silence I heard from Him. I remember feeling alone in this mess. Did God hate me? Was I the one human that He had finally turned his back on? The one that he said, *"I have had enough of you!"*? Was I the one he had forsaken?

Laying in the bed smelling her on the sheets and the pillow. Reaching for her hand every night when I would go to bed. I was empty and alone. My blessing was gone, I had destroyed her and our family. Every time I look at my daughter, I would see her stepmom, every time I would look at my little dude, I would see his mom. Close my eyes, and there she was.

Everywhere I looked I would see her, but it was not her. She was not there. I lost her.

The only thing I could focus on was her, and the mistakes I was making and had made. How could I fix anything, where would I start? I would get so pissed and angry at myself, I just wanted to disappear. Leave everything and everyone. I was ashamed of who I was, what I had done, everything. How could I live with myself? So much hate building up in my heart. All directed at me.

Over the past 41 years of my life, I have gained a lot and lost much more. I have hurt a lot, and I have hurt a lot of people a lot more. Like I said, "some kind of monster". The one thing I have not lost is hope though. I have been able to hold onto that one for years. I had been told many times that I was going to do great things in my life, one day I would help people out, that I would inspire others. I like the sound of that, helping people, doing great things, but how?

Quick question, who likes rollercoaster rides? I do. The speed, the fear, the rush, the adrenalin of it all. So, come with me on the rollercoaster ride I call my life. Hop on in, buckle your safety belts, and remember to keep your arms and legs inside the... you know what? Forget the rules for a little bit and let's just enjoy this journey of ups and downs together.

F.M.L

F.M.L.

Chapter 1

Introducing... Me

In an attempt to not put you to sleep I will do my best to quickly tell you about me. A little bit of history to get to know me. I was born in the Summer of 1978 the day before my mom's birthday. I guess you could say it was a great birthday present for my mom. Funny thing is that I was born 22 days late, my due date was my parents' wedding anniversary, so I guess you could say I was always a bit of a procrastinator from the start. My parents were both smart and hardworking people.

Apparently, a lot of people thought I was a girl, although my mom would dress me in stereotypical boy colors. People would say to her, "Oh my she is a pretty little girl", and things like that.

I had an older brother too which was always cool. Even though from what I remember, he wanted a little sister, he seemed to always take care of me and protect me. I remember my parents telling me something about how his friends had sisters so he thought all he would get was a sister too. According to mom, when she told him I was a boy he was more excited about that then having a little sister.

I always thought it was cool that my parents were high school sweethearts. Dad was a nerd, and mom was a cool hippie that missed Woodstock by a few short years. My mom was a stay at home mom in charge of raising two very smart, and strong-willed boys, while dad went off and worked hard to provide for us all. He worked in the nuclear power industry. I remember he had a blue hard hat which I thought was cool, not sure why I thought that. We lived close to family, both sets of grandparents, aunts, and uncles. I was even fortunate enough to live close to one of my great grandparents. Not all my family lived in the same state. My dad's parents were divorced so I got to see his father every so often as well as my dad's stepmom. He was young when they got divorced. So, I had some family that lived out of state, but it was great living around family and getting to see them. I did not understand what divorce was and how much pain it can cause people. I guess they all hid it very well too, or maybe just, over time they, got over it.

My parents had a fascination with J.R.R. Tolkien, you know "Lord of the Rings", "The Hobbit", I know my parents were nerds, but cool nerds. So much that we named all our dogs after characters from the books. We had a dog named Hobbit, but dad said we should have named him

Oscar the Grouch. My dog was a mutt, or missed bread, or designer dog... whatever they call them these days. Her name was Goldberry, even though there was not gold on her. Like I said my parents loved J.R.R. Tolkien. When I wasn't feeling good, she was there, when I was doing good, she was there. My mom told me that when I was not feeling well, and sleeping on the couch or something, Goldberry would curl up next to me the whole time I was sleeping. She lived up to the saying "man's best friend", but she was a boy's best friend to me.

We used to show dogs, go camping, went on some vacations here and there. It was cool because we got to go to Disney Land and Disney World, Knott's Berry Farms, things like that. We had a little popup trailer that we would pull behind my parent's yellow station wagon. Every time I see National Lampoons Summer Vacation and I see that big ugly green station wagon I think of my parent's car. They eventually upgraded to a new trailer that was larger and had bunk beds in the back. We would have sleepovers in the trailer with our friends. It was great.

As a kid, I thought everything was great in my life, which it was. Loving parents, awesome big brother, friends, and family all around. I went to school had fun, and just lived life as a kid. Had dogs, a nice little split entry house to live in, home-cooked meals, all the things a kid needed in life. We would go play "War" in the woods just at the end of the street, and there was a park at the bottom of the hill we would go to as well and play. If I had no one to play with, well I would just make up a game in my head and go play that, or just find something to do.

Now don't get me wrong we had issues like any other family. Money was not growing on trees in the back yard. I was not the perfect little kid that always did right and never got in trouble. My brother on the other hand, well he was perfect. At least that's what I thought every time I got in trouble, more like that is what I would say to my parents to try and deflect the attention off me. Looking back, he got in plenty of trouble too. I was just better at getting in trouble.

Around this time, I want to say I was about 5 maybe 6 years old when I was introduced to pornography. Yup, that's right, at the ripe old age of 5 or 6 years old my brothers' friends thought it would be fun to introduce me to porn. They had a stash of magazines in the woods at the top of the hill we lived on. I had no clue what I was looking at, but I was fascinated by it. The reaction of the older kids when they were looking at it, I didn't understand. They started to pick on me because I wasn't enthralled by it. Started asking me what was wrong with me, was I gay, did I like looking at guys and not girls.

Man, I was a fucking kid, I had no clue what was going on. I had no clue what looking at that stuff was going to do to me in the future. So, to show them I was cool, and "got it" I started to steal magazines for them. We would sit in the woods and look through them and make comments like we knew something we didn't. I did not realize it then, but I started looking at girls differently. This comes to hunt me later in life. It gave me a horrible idea of what women were and how they should be treated. It ruined my future relationships.

I also had a bit of a mouth on me. I tried to be cool so that the older kids, my older brother's friends, would like me more. I would steal some candy occasionally; I would also say vulgar words to get them to laugh and to show them how cool I could be. But overall, I think I was more annoying than anything else. I remember one day my mouth got me into some trouble. I don't remember what I said to the kid, he was a few years older than me, but he got mad, like really mad. I was riding my bike, and every time I would pass by him, I would call him a vulgar name and flip him the middle finger. After about the sixth time I think he was done. He ran up behind me and pushed me off my bike. I ended up flipping over the front of the handlebars and the reflector on the front of the bike rammed into my abdomen. It cut me deep, mom and dad had to take me to the emergency room.

There was another time where one of the kids we hung out with was picking on me. He was about a year maybe two older than me. My brother and his friends did not like that very much. So, one day they held him while I hit him. I don't really remember much about what was said or done. I just remember them holding him while I punched him with all my might. I felt bad after doing it, even though all my brothers' friends were cheering me on. The cool thing was a couple of days later we were all friends and playing. But that's how things were back then. Get into a fight with a friend, next day you are back together playing tag, or football in the yard. Again, it was good, things were good, life was good.

Then there was my first introduction to getting punched in the face. I was in elementary school, first or second grade, I know it was winter because I remember the kid putting on his gloves right before punching me. It was so stupid... we were on the playground when it happened. Just out of nowhere he walks up to me and asks if I liked this one girl. Now, remember this is like first or second grade... I said yes because we were friends. Next thing I know he rears back and then all a sudden.... BAM, he punches me right in the face. He then tells me that she was his girlfriend and to back off.

To be honest, I said yes because I liked her as a friend, I honestly had no clue what dating or being "girlfriend and boyfriend" was back then. I just stood there in shock, admittedly I did start to tear up and cry a bit, I mean come on he punched me the face for being friends with a girl! A bunch of kids laughed at me, so did the kid who punched me and his two friends that were with him. This is not the last time I got made fun of for crying. It happened here and there throughout my life.

One day when I was about 7 my dad got laid off from the company he was working for. Again, something I did not really get it. I just knew that dad had to go get a new job. Which he did, and that meant we had to move, from the North East all the way to the great North West.

Dad picked a job up with a computer software company. It was a long shot for them, but they made the choice to move, a huge leap of faith. Little did we know what would happen with this tiny software company, and how that would be such a great thing for my parents and the family.

So, dad moved out to start his job, and we followed shortly after. Mom had to get the house packed and some things sold off. I think it was January 1, 1986, the three of us were off to the airport to move out to the great northwest to start a new chapter in our lives.

Chapter 2

Hello Seattle

See already on to chapter 2, or "the next chapter". Well, there we were, landing at the airport. Dad was there to pick us up and take us to our new home. New schools, new friends, new houses, all that stuff. We lived there for about seven years before we moved again, which I'll get into later.

Things were tight for my parents and stressful, to begin with. We were living in a condo, which sounds fancy and all, but the company dad worked for was paying for it. I couldn't tell at the time that they were stressed out; they hid it well. We were broke, I guess, I didn't know we were, but mom and dad stayed positive around my brother and me.

I think we had been living in the great Northwest for a couple of years when we found out that our great-grandpa had passed, my dad's grandpa. It hit dad and my brother hard. I knew that him dying meant I would not see him ever again. But his death did not bring out that emotion of pain or grieving with me. I was young, so I am guessing that is it.

During those seven years in Washington, we moved homes about four times. As dad's work situation got better, he made sure our lifestyle got better. I remember when I was in fourth grade, my brother was in sixth grade, he would get bullied. I am talking beat down by some of the kids at school. He was always bigger than me, but for some reason, he did not like to fight. Me on the other hand, well, I didn't mind fighting.

I had my fair share of being picked on and being bullied. When I would go to my dad about it, I would get brushed off and told "I mean whatever happened to "sticks and stone may break my bones, but names will never hurt me"? I would get told I needed to have thicker skin, and I needed to get over it. Anyway, it was not the best feeling being called names and made fun of nor was it fun getting told to get over it. I remember getting into a few fights here and there. Sometimes my brothers' friends, you know "the older kids", would cheer me on and give me pointers on how to beat someone up. Something about letting all the frustration out and anger out felt good. Then I would see the other kid crying and hurt and I felt horrible for having caused that.

I guess my parents got sick of it because about mid-year my brother and I got pulled out of school and my mom started to home school us. Man getting to stay home all day, get my schoolwork done quickly, then off to play Nintendo, what a life. Then my brother and I started delivering newspapers in the afternoon. Man, now I was making money, I was loving it.

We went to church just about every Sunday, my brother and I went to a boy scout's kind of thing every Wednesday evening. It was fun hanging out with other kids, seeing as I lost a few friends when I got pulled out of school to be homeschooled.

It was a large church, the building was huge to me, and there were so many people. I remember sitting in church, falling asleep every Sunday. I could not focus on it, I did not get it, but I went because well, I was a Christian and Christians went to church every Sunday and on Christmas Eve, right? I didn't get the whole relationship with God. I remember when my brother got baptized. I remember sitting there thinking "man that is so cool, all these people are here to see my brother get baptized." I again had no clue what that was all about, nor did I care. I just wanted to do it because people would see me. There were a few kids at the church that would call me names or pick on me at times. That seemed to happen a lot in my life. I would get upset over it. I would just remember "sticks and stones…." and move along.

A lot of people my parents hung out with were from dad's work or church. I remember hearing stories from a lot of them about how God showed up in their life, or at a moment, and how He provided for them. I was like "Umm what do you mean? You are rich you provide for you". I know I was not that bright when it came to that kind of thing. I remember a story that one of mom and dad's friends told us, I will call her Mrs. B. for this story. Mrs. B said it was proof that God exists and cared about us. She lived on a lake with her family and every day she would go for a morning swim. She said how her dog, a beautiful German Shepard if I remember correctly, would always follow her by walking up and down the boat dock that they had. Well, this one day she was swimming and she stopped to talk to the dog. She said something was different about the way the dog was looking at her that day.

In a flash, the dog jumped in the lake right on top of her and was basically "attacking" her for lack of a better word. She told us that she knew nobody was around, there was never anyone around at that time of day. While this was happening, she remembers being underwater with the dog. fighting to get him off her. She could see the dock from under that water, no one was there. She looked again and saw a lady jumping in the water after her. This lady grabbed the dog and helped Mrs. B. get back on the dock. When Mrs. B. looked around there was no sign of anyone having been there. The dock was made of wood and yet there was no sign of that the other lady had been there. Mrs. B. looked to see if the lady was still in the water, but nothing. The lady was gone. Mrs. B. told me it had to have been an angel.

Over the years I heard more stories like this from my parent's friends again about how God had shown up to save them in certain situations. I was like "Whatever!!!", that's not what God does, maybe back in the Bible days sure, but not now.

Being homeschooled kind of sucked too, be honest. Mom could turn anything into a lesson. School was just about every day it seemed because of that. I didn't have many friends because all the kids that lived around us went to school and I didn't, so I was "not normal". I mean there were a couple of kids that would hang out, but if a friend from their school wanted to hang out, they would leave me for them.

There was one "friend" that I had from school that I hung out with. He was a little odd, to be honest looking back. Here is another situation of my life that was not, well the healthiest. I used to hang out with him on weekends. I never thought anything of it, but he never wanted to hang at my house. He always wanted me to spend the night at his place. I was cool with it for the most part. He had an older sister, she was like 18 or 19, I was about 10 or 11, I think. He used to have wigs in his room, he claimed that they were his sisters. I never thought anything of it, I mean we were friends why would he lie? One night I remember I was spending the night at his place like I frequently did.

This night was different though, he was acting strange to me. We went to his room and just started talking like we always did. He put on one of his "sisters" wigs and started telling me to call him by his sisters' name and he started acting like he was his sister. After a while, I fell asleep. That night I woke up, I slept on the floor most of the time when I was over there, and I noticed he was on the floor with me. He had his hands wrapped around me, and up my shirt on my chest. I remember just being there on the floor wondering with the hell was going on. I felt very uncomfortable, so I moved, well I got up and went to the bathroom. When I came back, he was in his bed. I honestly through I had imagined the entire thing. So, I went right back to sleep. After that, every time I went over it just got even stranger with him and his actions. Another night I woke up and he was doing the same thing, this time his hands went down my pants. He was talking to me this time. He was telling me to pretend he was his sister and that this was okay because we were nest friends. I freaked out and jumped up off the floor and went to the bathroom again. This time I was scared, I had no clue what was going on. What was my best friend doing? Why was he touching me there? Why was he rubbing me that way? It took me a moment before I could go back into the room. When I got back to the room, again, he was in his bed.

My dad never really liked this friend, he always just told me "something was wrong with him." and I always thought my dad was just a jerk and didn't like any of my friends. During this time of my life, I was already being called gay by family members and some of the kids in the area. I was really wondering what the hell was wrong with me. Why was I such an outcast? Why were people always asking me if I was gay, and calling me a homo? The last time I spent the night at this guy's house was the worst. Again, waking up to him touching me. This time he was kissing me telling me how much he loved me. I told him to stop and when I turned around, he was wearing a wig, and in his sister's underwear.

He told me again it was normal, and it was just a game. He said it didn't mean anything and to just let him do this. I noticed my shorts had been pulled down and he was holding my... well, I think you get the picture I don't need to spell it out. He told me that this was what best friends do, best friends that cared about each other. He told me not to tell anyone about this, I begged him to stop, but he wouldn't. Honestly, I was scared, I didn't know what to do. I could not call my parents they wouldn't understand. I pushed him off and slept in the bathroom. When my parents came to get me, I got in the car and didn't say anything to them. I never told them what happened, I mean how could I? Everyone was calling me gay; I didn't think I was because I liked girls, and I didn't like what he was doing to me. I think this is really the first time I took all my emotions and pushed them down as deep as I could to hide things from people.

I started to steal magazines again to see if that would start doing anything for me to make me feel like I was into girls. I went on a rampage with this. Every month I would steal several magazines I didn't care which one it was, as long as it had girls in it. I had them stashed in every corner of my room, under my bed everything. Every night I would look through them.

Let's fast forward a bit, I remember one day my folks went to an event of some kind for the weekend, my brother was old enough to take care of us at that point. We had a list of chores to do while mom and dad were gone.

Sometimes they would have a family friend watch us, then they started to just have them drop in and check on us. This time it was just the two of us, lots of food in the house, sodas to drink, games to play, and chores. In typical fashion, I started getting on my brother's last nerve. Calling him names and just being a little jerk to him.

It was cold and wet outside, and we were raking up the leaves because that was on the chore list. We were both in a bad mood I guess, I was not really working as hard as he was, and I am sure that's why he was mad. I was mad because it was cold and wet out and I just wanted to go play Nintendo. So, I started getting into it with him, calling him names, and making fun of him. He had finally had enough of it. He grabbed the rake and threw it at me. He was about twenty feet away from me, seemed like a hundred that day. It all happened in a flash, one second I was laughing at him and calling him names, the next I was hit in the face with a rake. He says he told me to jump because the rake started to fall towards the ground. I heard "duck", so I did. I still wonder today if he really did say jump or if I heard right and he said duck?

I was freaking out. My face had just been smashed in by a huge rake from a hundred feet away. It felt like a Mac Truck had just smashed into my face. I was hit so hard in the head that my grandchildren will feel it. Tears streaming down my face, I couldn't breathe, I could see, I could talk. Some of you would be ticked off at your older sibling and ran and told on them. Not my brother and I. Nope, after I started breathing again, and stopped seeing stars we came up with a plan. We came up with the best story ever so mom and dad would never find out that this happened. That's right, we blamed it on the dogs and cats. We told our parents that we were just doing our thing, and I tripped over the dogs and cats and fell down the stairs.

My brother and I always had each other's backs when it came down to it. Yes, we got into fights, we called each other names, we even punched the crap out of each other at times. But the fact is we loved each other and cared for each other. Therefore, we protected each other. Oh, and by the way, that story about tripping over the animals lasted for years. Now I am not advocating lying, especially not to your parents because one day they will find out. They always find out.

I spent a lot of time trying to be cool so that people would like me. I would make some stories out to be larger than they really were. I would try to get the clothes that all the "cool kids" wore. I remember one time I wanted Air Jordan's, I had to have them. All the cool kids had them and I had to be cool, besides dad had the money.

Well, remember how I told you all that my parents could turn anything into a lesson? This was no different. My dad pointed out that I had a job and I made money. I didn't get it. I mean dad had to buy me shoes. He was my dad and that is what parents do. They buy their kids what they want. Dad took this time to explain that he had already provided me with shoes, and he did just a few weeks earlier. But he just didn't understand, my money was for Nintendo games, not shoes. He told me that I would need to make a choice between the video game I wanted or the shoes. I didn't understand then that all he was trying to help me do was learn that sometimes we have to make choices and budget for the things we want. Not everything would come easy and sometimes I would have to work harder to get everything I wanted. This lesson continued to come up all throughout my life. In case you really wanted to know, I got the shoes and they did not make me cooler, and I had to do some extra chores so I could get that video game I wanted too.

I learned a lot of real-life lessons while being homeschooled, like how to budget, how to pay taxes, how to tithe and what amount to tithe. Still didn't fully understand that whole walk with Jesus thing. But I would put my couple of dollars in the basket on Sunday's because I "had to". I learned how to buy a car, and negotiate the price down, paying cash versus financing. Why you want a savings account and a checking account. They were really setting me up for success as an adult so that I would never have to go through what they went through as a young couple with kids. Don't worry, they also taught me the normal school curriculum.

I took piano lessons, even though I really wanted to play guitar. I got enrolled in a small performing arts school a few minutes away. That was fun because I got to do plays and learn how to act. I was good at acting up, but this was better because I got in less trouble. Oh, and I finally got to take guitar lessons as well. I wanted to learn how to rock out on the electric guitar and play rock music. I was starting to get into rock and heavy metal at this time. I loved music, it spoke to me, I guess. I could listen to music and be like "I know how that feels" or "man this song is so relatable to me...". I would listen to music all day if I could, and at night I would fall asleep to the radio playing some sort of heavy metal music.

Finally, mom and dad signed me up for guitar lessons, classical guitar, but it was still guitar lessons. They wanted me to learn how to read sheet music and actually play songs. Again, I just wanted to thrash on a guitar like Slash from Guns and Roses, or James Hatfield from Metallica. I also liked some Hip hop as well, and some classic rock like the Doors, Steppenwolf, Iron Butterfly, Led Zeppelin, stuff like that. In a nutshell, I still can't play the guitar.

One morning my mom, brother, and I went to our favorite bakery, a friend of my parents owned it. I, not so politely, told my mom at breakfast that I was never going to use fractions. There was no possible way normal people needed to know this information, and that it was just stupid and mean that she was forcing me to learn how to add, subtract, multiply, and divide these stupid fractions. Again, I had a mouth on me, and while my parents have always told me a was a good kid and respectful, I think I pushed the limits to the max.

Well, mom jumped on this opportunity to show me I was dead wrong. If I remember correctly, she pointed out all the food in the bakery and pointed out I liked to eat it. I, of course, agreed, because it was all amazing. She then called the owner over and told him what I had said about fractions. Needless to say, I ended up learning how none of that stuff could be made if he didn't know how to add, subtract, multiply, and divide fractions. And if he didn't then his business would not exist, and I could not have any of the food there that I like. So again, mom won.

We still had a bunch of dogs, and a couple of them had puppies. It was one of my responsibilities to put the dogs out, feed them, and clean up after them. At one point a couple of the dogs got really sick, while under my watch. Admittedly I did not take that good of care of them. I did the minimum needed. I did not care about the food was on the floor or in the bowl. If they had food, it was good. I loved having dogs, I just didn't want to have to take care of them. But when these dogs got sick, and my parents got mad, I felt like I was being blamed for the dogs being sick. So, I hated taking care of the dogs even more. I started hating the dogs, I just didn't care about them. If they died, they died.

Truth be told, my parents never blamed me for the dogs getting sick, even when a dog died, I was not blamed on it. In my head, I took everything my parents said as they were blaming me. I had my pity parties and lashed out at them. I guess I knew I was not taking care of the dogs the way I was supposed, and guilt was kicking in. There were a lot of times when I would get in trouble for doing something wrong and I would blow it out of proportion and act like my parents hated me or loved my brother more because "he never got in trouble'.

My brother at fifteen, being homeschooled and smart, took his GED and graduated so to speak at that time. He wanted to work and go to college. Me on the other hand, I just wanted to go back to school with the normal kids, make friends, and be "normal", be accepted by everyone, and not be made fun of by kids my age. I didn't want to feel like an outcast, like a freak, like something was wrong with me. I messed up a lot, got myself into trouble on the regular. Looking back, I was a normal kid. I just didn't know it at the time.

During all of this, I started taking Karate, as a form of physical education so to speak. For me, it was because I wanted to be the Karate Kid or a Ninja. I started studying martial arts at a young age, around nine maybe ten years old. It was great, I was doing something I loved, and I was good at it. From the very first class, I took I knew that this was going to be a huge part of my life. Plus, I was one step closer to be the Karate Kid or a Ninja. The best part was I got to fight people, and not get in trouble for and not feel bad for having gotten into a fight.

One-day dad came home and talked to mom about some opportunity his job had offered him. Looked like we were getting ready to move again. This time it was not because they let dad go, and this time we got to pick where we were moving to. The options were back to the east coast, North Carolina, or head south to Texas. Well, we had family in the south, so we decided to move there to be closer to his dad and stepmom and his grandma.

My dad and brother drove the motorhome down to our new home before mom and I went down. Mom had to stay behind and sell the house; finish packing and make sure the movers got everything taken care of and on its way down south. One day my mom asked me to turn her car around in the driveway, we were getting ready to load up a bunch of food and go donate it to a shelter for the holidays. I had seen my parents and brother do this a million times, I got this. Well no I didn't. I was so busy thinking I was cool and how I was driving that I did not notice the neighbors' boat trailer sticking out. It was ok, the car let me know it was there. That's right, I just ripped the front bumper off my mother's Cadillac. Man, I just messed up again, "like I always". Well that was what I told myself.

Needless to say, mom was not happy, and I was never going to be allowed to drive until I was eighteen. I just couldn't stop messing up, in my mind. Everything was my fault in my head, and my parents were so mean. At least that is what I had been telling myself for a while. Never really looking at what I was doing to cause any of it, now trust me I got in plenty of trouble with my parents, I just didn't see at the time that it was my doing. This is when the self-talk started to get to me, you know the whole "you're no good, you will never be good enough" the belief that I was not as good as my brother at anything.

Chapter 3

The Lone Star State

*N*ow that my brother, dad, and I were down South, living in an apartment while mom took care of everything up north, and they closed on the house down South. Dad got me enrolled in school, I started looking for another martial arts school to go to. I was about fourteen at this point, it was mid-year of ninth grade, and I was going back to public school. This was exciting for me, things were going to be awesome, and I was going to be normal again. No more homeschooling.

When mom got everything taken care of up North, she moved down with us. We got moved into the new home, and man it was nice. My brother and I kind of had the whole second floor to ourselves. Pool table, big screen TV, surround sound system... it was just amazing.

The first day of school, a fresh start, time to make friends, the new kid in class, same old "bullies". I was still different; I was still odd. I did not dress like the rest of the kids; I never had good fashion sense and still don't. I had no clue how to use a padlock for my locker, and the people around me had no issue making fun of me for that.

The transition from being homeschooled to going back to public school really wasn't that bad. I remember one week, I think it was my second week in school, every day after lunch these two guys would run up behind me and hit me as they ran past while laughing at me. Calling me names like "fagot", "homo", making fun of how I was dressed. There was another kid who would sit down with me at lunch who would steal my fries. One day he told me there was nothing I would do about it because I was too much of a pussy to do anything about it. Something kind of snapped right then and there with me. I grew some balls. Everyone at that table was laughing about it, and I watched him go for my fries, as he went for more fires I grabbed his hand and the back of his head and pinned his head on the table and force-fed him a couple of fries. I finally started to stand my ground that day.

Things were getting normal for me I guess you could say. Nothing dramatic really happened during that year at school. I made friends that I hung out after school. I was feeling normal and accepted. I no longer felt like a freak or an outcast. Summer break couldn't come fast enough.

That summer I lost contact with a lot of my friends from school. There was one guy I hung out with all summer though. He was one of the first guys I became friends with at school, we had algebra together. He introduced me to a bunch of great guys that summer. We all had that dumb 90's "grunge" haircut going on, you know, long hair that was split down the middle with the sides and back of our heads shaved. We hung out just about every day at this apartment community. We also hung out at the pool and played sand volleyball.

Most of these guys were a year or two older than me. Due to my birthday, I was normally the youngest kid in my class. But this worked because, like my brother, they all could drive. It seemed perfect, they all liked older cars, and drove them, as well as had motorcycles. We all liked the same kind of music, movies, cars, everything... we all just meshed so well. We looked like a bunch of skater punks, but they were good people. Most of them were Christians, but I had no clue that they were. They never really talked about it, looking back they just walked the walk and would lead by example.

My parents, brother, and I started going to church as a family again, but this time it was just one service. So, it wasn't as mundane for me. Every Sunday I would get dressed in a suit and tie, not by choice, and went off to church. Every time I would start to nod off to sleep when the Preacher would start preaching. He told some funny jokes and tried to make it fun, but it just didn't click with me. I didn't feel anything when I was there.

I would walk around and tell people I was a Christian; I mean I kind of was, I guess. I believed in God, I believed in Jesus, but still no relationship there. It was more like an insurance policy for me. I would tell people "Well I would rather waste my life believing in Him and find out there is nothing, rather than not believe in Him and find out He is real." I would pray when things were bad, or I wanted something bad and I wanted it to turn out better. I treated God as my personal genie in a lamp.

That summer was great, just hanging out and having fun, and just doing some stupid stuff. One time some friends and I thought it would be a good idea to ride down the hill in a recycling bin. We were over at a friend's house who lived at the top of a little hill. We get one of those little blue recycling bins out and sat in it. Then we grabbed ahold of the back of my buddy's motorcycle while he started driving down the hill. We let go of the bike and rode down the hill, in the street mind you, in the bin. We each took turns... It was my turn now.

I hopped in, put the helmet on, grabbed the back of the bike, and off he went. He lifted his hand in the air to let me know that it was time to let go and enjoy the ride down the hill. I heard this voice in my head saying, "Stand up and ride this bin down the hill...", this is more metaphorically speaking... I didn't hear voices in my head, and I am almost positive this was not God speaking to me... just a stupid idea I had. But I did it, not worrying about balance, or the speed I may have achieved going down this hill. Not caring about the fact that I was in a little plastic blue box. Nope, none of that mattered... What mattered was me trying to impress my friends and looking cool.

I started to stand up, I was almost there. Wind blowing in my face as I raced down the hill, like a surfer on a wave.

Boom, there it was... now I was not standing up in the bin looking awesome sliding down the hill. Boom, there was a rock in the street and the bin hit it, throwing me out of the recycling bin onto the street. In a flash, I thought I was going to die, or break bones. Next thing I knew I hit the ground, tumble down the street. Oh, and I was in shorts and a short-sleeve shirt, and to top that all off I didn't really strap the motorcycle helmet on properly. The wind got knocked out of me, the helmet flew off my head, and I slid down the street a few feet. When my body stopped donating my flesh to the concrete, and I could catch my breath, I started to stand up. Nothing was broken, I was alive. Then it hit, right there as I stood up... nope, not that God saved me from dying or breaking my bones, not that he saved me from cracking my skull open on the street after the helmet flew off my head. What hit me right then and there was the pain from all the scratches up and down my body from sliding several feet. See I never was good at giving God credit for saving me.

My parents were not too impressed with this story when I got home that day. For some reason they never seemed impressed with me when I did something stupid or bad, go figure right. That also is one of many stories I could tell you all about myself, but I really don't think you want to hear about all the times I did something stupid and got hurt. I'm just wanting you to know that my childhood was a normal one for the most part.

Summer was ending and school was about to start back up, moving on to High School. Right after school started, I had my 15th birthday and my folks got me a scooter.

That's right, I drove a 50cc scooter to and from school and work. I felt so liberated and independent being about to drive as well as start making money again. Little did I know that this scooter also made me a target for getting picked again. Now the point here is not that I got picked on or bullied, the point is how I allowed it to start affecting me. I got called nerd, dork, fag, gay, loser... the list goes on and on. These same kids that called me names would try to run me off the road sometimes. I was about a year younger than a lot of people in my grade, so they had their driver's license that year while I was working on getting my drivers permit. I started letting that stuff bury itself into my head. I started to believe it, and it made me mad. Like mad about everything, and mad at everyone. I kept that all buried deep inside so that I would look happy on the outside.

Everything would just piss me off quick, I started thinking that nobody liked me. I thought they only hung out with me because of my brother, or something like that. And yes, that made me sad, it would build up anger. Then I would feed that anger and sadness with horrible self-doubt. If I got a bad grade and my parents talked to me about I would lash out at them and say things like I was sorry I wasn't as smart as my brother or something childish like that, which would just feed that anger more. I don't know how to explain it that well, but I would go from positive to negative quick, over the dumbest things, and have these ridiculous thoughts over nothing. You know just getting all bent out shape about it and then boom, right back to positive.

So, anyway, it was a typical year of school, work, sleep, then on the weekends hanging out with friends. I know very normal, nothing special and exciting... nothing newsworthy. I had a few girlfriends here and there. Normally I was the one who got dumped, you know the old story... "Oh, you're like my best friend." Or "It's not you, it's me." And then there was the "You're too nice of a guy to be with a girl like me...", I don't even know what that one really means. Each rejection just made me feel a bit more worthless and made me think something was wrong with me. Mostly because I would tell myself those things.

I say all of this to just show you I really had a normal life. Most people go through this kind of stuff and have no issues with it at all. I just allowed small things to consume me, small bits of sadness or anger would be allowed by me to take over my heart. It was almost a daily thing for me to tell myself "They are right you are a loser; you suck. Nobody really likes you man, they like your brother." I think anger and sadness are just hungry little animals inside our heads that want to be fed, we can feed them and help them grow, or not. It really is up to us. Too bad I didn't think that way back then because this type of stuff comes to bite me in the butt later in life.

Chapter 4

<u>Church Camp</u>

I really am trying to wrap this part of my life up fast for you all. I am sure you are wondering what the point is of all of this... I am not sure. I just wanted you all to get to know me, I guess. So, let's keep this story going and see if you get anything out of it.

One day one of my best friends from school, Cory, invited me to go to a church camp with him over the weekend. Well, I wasn't doing anything that week, so I was like "sure let's go". I had never been to a church camp before, but I loved camping, so I was game. I had gone to church with him a couple of times, he was the only one that ever invited me to the church in high school. We met when I first started going back to public school, we had English, Science, and Health class together that year. Honestly, he was more of a brother to me than a friend.

So, we meet up at his church parking lot to go to this church camp, I was such a punk at that time. I think I had a shirt on that said something to the effect of:

"It's not whether you win or lose, it's whether the cheerleaders show up."

Classy, I know right? But that was the kind of person I was. I also had a shirt with a little skull engulfed in flames, and the back of that one said something really snarky and sarcastic too. Most of my shirts back then were sarcastic, snarky, rude, or arrogant. It was the year of No Fear t-shirts. He introduced me to the youth leaders that were going with us for the weekend and to some of his friends. I already knew a few of the people that were going because we went to school together.

Everyone was nice and even the youth leaders seemed excited to meet me. It was almost too nice of a feeling like I didn't know what to do. I started looking for opportunities to be sarcastic and to be honest just rude. Still trying to be cool, instead of just letting people like me for who I was. At one point when the youth leaders asked me if I had found Jesus? I popped off with "I didn't know he was lost". You know because I had to try and be funny, I need to make people laugh and distract them from anything going on within me.

Being that this was my first time going to a church camp, I had no idea what to expect. I had heard stories from people about how "God just showed up…" and "He changed them that day…". I didn't expect Him to "show up" or "show Himself to me". I just wanted to hang out with a friend at a campsite and have fun. I will admit that the entire time I was there, every time we would pray, I would just close my eyes and act like I was involved. When the youth leaders would say "Repeat after us..." I would repeat what they were saying, but it was just words to me. It didn't move me, I didn't feel the presence of God, I didn't feel changed... I just felt like plain old me. For the most part, I did feel good, I was happy, and I really didn't have the urge to talk bad about myself.

The youth leaders really didn't talk to me that much at the campsite. I think mainly because I was very off-putting when they tried to talk to me on the way to the camp. Also, I didn't help matters that much with my attitude, like I was better than them.

One of them did at one point pull me aside to talk. I don't really remember much of what he said, but I do remember him asking why I was so sarcastic about everything. He pointed out to me that Jesus loved me, and that I did not have to try so hard to be funny or cool all the time. Well, of course, that ticked me off, I wasn't trying hard at anything... That was just "who I was". I think I even told him that too. He asked why I was there, so I told him simply "Ummm... Because I was invited". That was the last time any of the youth leaders really talked directly to me. I don't blame them at all.

I didn't realize it at the time but looking back at my time spent at camp I can remember feeling loved. Not like my family didn't love me, or anything like that. It was calming while I was there. I can only explain now as the presence of God was there, and it was His love that I was feeling.

Maybe I just didn't want to admit it then, or I just didn't understand it then, or just wasn't ready for it, I really don't know.

When we drove back home from the camp, I started feeling guilty about the way I had acted as well as the way I talked to the youth leaders. Those feelings hit me the second we left the campgrounds. A lot of shame filled my heart, then anger towards myself. The words started swimming around my head. There I was feeding that little anger monster again, and he loved what I was serving up. I would have these little battles in my head a lot. Like in the cartoons where the white angel would pop up on one shoulder, then the red devil on the other both talking in my ears. Normally I would brush the angel off, to be honest, but that didn't happen this time. I also remember feeling like I missed out on an opportunity at that camp. I was focused on having fun, and not listening to what was being said and taught.

When we got back to the church, we piled up in a friend's car and headed out to eat. Everything was good... No more, "Had I found Jesus?", no more questions about my faith or religion. Just time to be "me" and go have fun. Little did I know what impact that trip really had on me, and how I would be able to reflect on things years later.

I remember we all went out that afternoon to grab something to eat. It was a nice sunny morning so when we were driving the windows were down, A/C was one. When we sat down to eat, we noticed that the weather was getting bad, it started raining bad, then the hail started coming down. I am not talking about little pea-sized hail, you know the kind the kids love to run to the window and watch, I am talking about hail the size of a baseball. We remembered that the windows were down on the car... So, me being the "nice guy" I was I grabbed the keys and ran out to the car to roll the windows up. As I was running back into the restaurant, in the hailstorm, I got nailed in the back of the head by a huge chunk of ice. Maybe God was trying to tell me something, maybe he was trying to wake me up. All I knew at that point was my head hurt, bad. I look back now, and I bet it was God trying to wake me up.

Chapter 5

<u>High School</u>

The last few years of high school were good. By this point in time, things were good for mom and dad. Not really having to worry about finances like a lot of parents had to do. Nice house, nice cars, living in a nice town, and I was going to a nice school. Pretty basic stuff right, I mean what could I have gone through that could cause me to write a book, let alone a book that could have some sort of message for someone out there? It's coming... I hope.

I remember when it was coming up to my sixteenth birthday, the words my mom had told after wrecking her car... "You are not driving until you are 18". All my friends had cars, they were all driving, and I wanted that freedom, that privilege, so bad. Good thing my parents were kind, loving, and forgiving parents. Not sure what I did, or how I earned it, but they allowed me to take driver education classes, which meant I was going to be allowed to get my license. Oh man the joy that filled me when they signed me up, it was amazing. I dreamt of getting an old Mustang all my life, all 16 years of it at that point. My parents said that if I kept my grades up, they would help me get a car, and get insurance for me; I just had to pay for gas.

I knew I would get that 1964 ½ Red Mustang, with a black convertible top, black interior, with a 289 V8. It was going to look like it had just rolled off the showroom floor, completely perfect in every way. My 16th birthday was right around the corner, and I wondered... "How would mom and dad get the car to the house for me?", "Would I come home from school and see it sitting on the driveway, or maybe it would be in the garage?" Got home from school, and no Mustang in the driveway, no Mustang in the garage. I just knew that we would be going out on the weekend to get it. I mean come on, dad had money, they gave my brother a cool older car, why wouldn't they get me my Mustang?

Well, I didn't get a Mustang, I would later find that they would mess with me and give a model of a Mustang, I think they even gave me a Matchbox car. What I did was an old, bright yellow, 1970's, British sports car that needed a lot of work. As in it really didn't even run, I am not sure it was even legally allowed on the road at that point. I looked like a wedge of cheese; it was at one time my brother's car that he never got running. Lesson here for any teens reading this is... just because your parents can afford to buy you something doesn't mean that you deserve it, you really must earn it. I had earned the privilege to drive, I had not earned the privilege of having my dream car bought for me.

I put a lot of work into that car to get it up and running. I had to do some electrical work on it and had little clue as to what I was doing, but I got it running. I even gave it a new paint job. Don't get excited, I went to the local Kmart and bought spray paint, yellow spray paint, and just hosed it down. The electrical system was working, but man the wiring was a rat's nest by the time I was done with it. But I was driving MY car. One time, I think this was during my senior year in high school when I went to take my SAT's the car caught on fire on the way to the test, and on the way back home. Eventually, my parents helped me get a better, safer vehicle. It was great because it never caught on fire, and I didn't have to flip an extra switch to turn on the reverse lights when I was backing up like my first car.

Again, in an effort, to move my childhood story on a little faster let's just jump ahead a bit, mainly because I don't want to talk about my SAT scores. Please note that I said scores… Most get an SAT score, nope not me. I had to take it twice, the first time I got an 850, which I think you get for spelling your name right on the test. To my defense, I had been out late the night before at my first concert. I remember it so well; Bush, Toadies, and Hum, it was fantastic. Okay, okay…. so maybe not a great reason to get that low of a score, but there was also the car catching on fire thing there too. I can't really tell you what happened the second time I took the test, but it was another 850. These two scores took me right back into the "I am no good, I am stupid like everyone says I am" phase.

To be honest, I am not sure who everybody was that was saying this stuff, it wasn't like everyone in my life said this stuff to me every day. It happened a few times here and there, a little bit of bullying, and a few of the "cool kids" snubbing their noses at me because I guess I wasn't cool enough to be their friend. Regardless it was back, tearing myself down, insulting myself, and feeling worthless. Saying things to myself like "You're never going to be able to get into a college", "Why can't you be smarter like your brother?".

Now the crazy thing is, is that my brother and I had a fantastic relationship. He was much better at things than I was, he was much smarter, or maybe he just applied himself better at things than I did. Any time I needed help he was there to help. Even if he and I were in a fight if anyone did anything to me... watch out! I remember a few times where he and I would be in a fight, I mean a big fight. Actually punching each other, not just calling each other names, but trying to cause mass amounts of damage to each other... one of his friends started to jump in on the action. My brother turned around, and in so many words, let his friend know to never touch me again. This even applies to us today. But he was my protector so to speak. I could go to him for anything, tell him everything, and he never judged me. He would always give me advice and direction, even if it meant telling me something I didn't want to hear, but maybe needed to hear.

With all this being said I would still talk down to myself a lot. And why you may ask? I have no clue, to be honest, it was just something I did. My life was good, not perfect, but good. I guess I just felt like I was not good enough. I was not as good as my brother in my eyes, not as smart, not as strong, not as cool as him... again this was in my eyes. Every time I tried to be like him, I would fail and get down on myself. I finally started to see that I was me and my brother... well he was not me and I was not him. I guess you could say I was finally finding myself, finding my groove.

My sophomore and junior years flew by so fast. Just kind of the average kid, average family... Average life. Got into Theater/Drama classes which were just amazing. I loved being able to get in front of people and entertaining them. Just something about being on stage, acting out a scene, or helping with the production of a play brought a lot of enjoyment to me. I loved how I would get nervous about getting in front of everyone, even just to try out, let alone perform.

For years I wanted to get into action, I had dreams of being a famous actor doing movies, traveling all over the world, receiving awards, and living the "good life". I figured action films would be the way I would go because of my martial arts background. Needless to say, that never happened. No Hollywood for me, no movies, not even a "Straight to VHS", sorry some of you might not know what a VHS tape is... how about not even a "Straight to DVD" deal. But doing theater in high school was good enough.

That was about the only thing that I got excited about in high school, regarding school, that is. School spirit was not that big of a focus for me. I couldn't have cared less about the football games, baseball games, homes coming games, or even the homecoming dance. The Friday pep rallies were great because I got out of class and hung out with my friends. Remember this was the 90's and I leaned more towards the grunge type attitude at that time. Not to the point where I was an outcast sitting by myself in the corner of the lunchroom. Just more the way I dressed, music I listened to, and view of a lot of people.

I remember meeting this one guy in English class, he found out from another friend of mine that I was into the martial arts, his name was Rich, don't ask me why... you really don't want to know. Well, Rich sat right behind me in class and would just annoy the crap out of me for about a week. I hadn't been bullied by anyone for about a year at this point, yet this guy kept saying how he wanted to beat me up, or how he could take me. He would hold his fist right in my face and tell me how he could break my nose so easily and there was nothing I could do to stop him. I told my brother about it, and he told me if I didn't kick the crap out of him, well he would. I didn't ever kick the crap out of Rich... he became one of my best friends that year in school.

Rich would always have a deck of cards; at lunch, he would be playing cards with people and take them for a few bucks here and there. Even in class, he would do it, I mean I didn't mind we always hung out and spent his winnings on the weekends. This kid would wear shorts and a short-sleeve shirt year-round, regardless of the weather.

Cory, Rich, and I would hang out all the time. Don't worry I had other friends that I hung out as well, but these two guys had a huge impact on me. Cory and I knew each other since ninth grade, Rich and I met in tenth grade. Regardless, we were best friends and hung out all the time, never got into trouble. They were more like brothers to me.

Some of my other friends were more into partying, smoking pot, drinking, things like that. For some reason, I never got into all that mess. It just wasn't my thing. It's not like it wasn't offered to me. The opportunities were there, right in front of me. I remember some kids buying pot in school, during class, or hiding around the corner outside to smoke a cigarette or whatever.

Moving on here, so school was going well, work was good, still had friends... good times, strong bonds. Still living the good life, at the same time still having a bad self-image for some reason. Dealing with fear as well. Fear of not doing good enough, fear of rejection, fear of letting my parents down, you know all the normal stuff that a lot of you deal with or have dealt with. Again, nothing special about me or my life. The thing for me was when things didn't go as planned, I would over analyze and find where I was to blame. Even if it was not my fault, I would take the blame. Maybe not verbally, but I would tell myself it was my fault. I would beat myself up a bit on the inside.

So, my junior year was coming to close, summer was almost upon us. After that, it would be my Senior year, the big time, the beginning to the end of my childhood.

That summer I did the usual, work and hang out with my friends and brother. One thing I did differently this summer was I would go workout at the gym with my brother and his friends. I was small, very lean and not that tall. Rich would go to the gym with us as well. I figured since I was going into my Senior year, I would try to make this huge change over the summer. You know come back a different person, be the guy that turned everyone's head. I think we were working out like three to five times a week. No matter how hard I worked, no matter how much I lifted, nothing seemed to change about me. I was still scrawny. Now I felt better, I had more energy, I was even eating more... A lot more. I think if I had wanted to, I could have shut a few All You Can Eat Buffets down, like make them go bankrupt. I couldn't stop eating, and even with that, I didn't grow in size. I guess getting jacked was not in my future. I would get frustrated, but it did not stop me from continuing to work out. It took me quite some time to just be happy with the way I looked and to be happy with who I was, but this was starting to happen in my life at this time.

I started to be good with who I was that summer, becoming more confident in me and liking myself. Not that I hated myself or anything like that, more just finding who I was and who I was going to be. That summer was a great growing experience for me. I can't pinpoint the exact time, or place, or situation that caused me to start feeling that way, it just started happening. I went to church a few times here and there with Cory, I even went on and off with my family. Again, those times in church were just feel good times for me, nothing learned and no connection.

Edward Bowers

My senior year started like any other year, my school had this thing where they played a Nine Inch Nails song every day for the first week of school, "Head Like a Hole". I remember the prior years I found it annoying, I was not going to bow down to anyone, and I was not going to get what I deserve. Yes, for those of us who lived through the '90s... we remember this song. For those of you who don't know it... I am sure you can go look it up. But this year, well I was the senior, and this song wasn't telling me to bow down. It had a different meaning to me this year. Funny how things have a meaning to you in your life at one time, then something changes, and it has a whole new meaning. Everything meant something different to me this year. I was more interested in school spirit than I ever had been, I was more engaged and prouder of my school. It was my last year of high school, my last year of childhood so to speak. I was feeling better about myself, better about things to come, I was ready for anything and everything.

Nothing exciting or detrimental happened the first semester, it was just good. I actually enjoyed going to school, I looked forward to school as much I looked forward to the weekends. My schedule was fantastic, I had early release which allowed me to work more, which meant more money in my account for the things I wanted. My parents taught me from an early age to work hard and save my money so that I could have the things I need and want. Having goals and dreams is very important and you needed to stay focused on them. One thing I wanted was that Mustang, remember I had that little, yellow, block of cheese, British "sports car". That four-cylinder engine was nothing compared to that V8 that was just sitting there in my dream Mustang, waiting for me to own. I had models of it, magazines with it, pictures of it... It was my lifelong goal to one day own that car; life long as in since I was a young teen. I had applied this rule my parents taught me several times in the past and I continue to try and apply even till today.

I am sure I have not done a great job explaining how I had a normal life so far. I just wanted to give you all a little bit of info. There was nothing really that major that happened back then. Just normal a normal life, with a loving family, and a few self-esteem issues that went away, dad made a lot of money and provided beautifully for us. It's not like I was addicted to drugs, getting arrested, or anything like that. Just a lot of school, work, having fun and sleep. My parents always provided a good life for my brother and I. They were always there for us, even when I thought they were not. In the chapters to come is when things get "interesting" so to speak. See I thought everything was going to be great for the rest of my life because I went to church most Sundays, oh don't forget I always went on Christmas Eve and Easter, so I had that going for my salvation too. I was making money and had some saved up too. I got good grades in school, followed the rules... Well most of the big ones, I would bend the small ones. I would not trade my childhood for anything, I would not go back and change anything.

Sure, I felt at times that my parents loved my brother more, but I think a lot of younger siblings go through that same phase. I would point out how they treated him differently than me and justify my thoughts based on that. It took me a while to learn that you can treat everyone the same because we are all different, but I was starting to understand that my Senior year. I also thought he was better at everything then I was, again I am sure a lot of younger siblings feel the same way. To be honest, he was better, and that was fine. I was not him and he was not me, and no matter how hard I tried to be something or someone different, I could not do it. I was me and that was a good thing. I guess maybe that is a small message here in this book, and maybe more to come. But just be happy with you and who you are. If you don't like the things you are doing, make those changes, but don't try to be someone else. Just make sure you are doing what it is right, don't hurt others just to make yourself feel better, and don't compare yourself. Set some goals and strive to reach them.

Oh, and I finally got rid of that yellow car, the death trap of fire and doom. I know you guys were really concerned about that. It was a relief for me. No more driving and having the electrical system fail on me at night, no more care catching on fire, no more sitting on the side of the road punching the steering wheel hoping that I could get it to start. Oh, and the gas gauge didn't work completely, so no more watching my miles to ensure I didn't run out of gas. Yes, I always kept a little gas can in the trunk, which was about all I could fit in the trunk of that car, so that when, not if, but when I ran out of gas I could make the hike to the closest gas station. You might be thinking "wait you said your dad made good or lots of money. Why did you drive such a POS?". I used to wonder the same thing. Everything throughout my life was a lesson. Dad provided what we needed, and he gave to my brother and me a lot of what we wanted. Somethings we had to earn with keep grades up, and some we had to earn our own money to get. There were times my mom and dad would split the cost with us. There were even times when I would earn the money to buy, and my parents would see that, and they would end up buying it for me. My parents always told me that I would appreciate things more if I earned them myself. They were right of course. I respected the things I was given, but when I earned it, through grades, or earning the actual money to get it, I respected the things even more.

Life lessons, gotta love them.

So, don't give up on reading the rest of the book, please. There might be something else you get out of what is to come.

Chapter 6

Being a Man?

Going back to school after Christmas break was like being at the top of a hill for me, you know you are at a high point, and you can see so much. It all looks wonderful. The first day back and seeing that Prom was coming, graduation was coming too. At the end of my childhood, adulthood was in my sights. This was so exciting for me. I saw myself getting into acting, competing in tournaments, becoming someone. No girlfriend, and to be honest I was perfectly fine with that. My luck in the past with girls was not that great. Most of them dumped me after about two weeks. Maybe a was a jerk to them, or maybe they were all right and we were better off as friends? I don't know, but I was fine with it.

Wouldn't you know it though, even though I was fine with no girlfriend, I met someone? We started dating, I know so cute, High School Sweethearts. I will call her my Ex, spoiler alert right here. Sorry to ruin it for you guys but this relationship does not turn out that great. A lot of great things happened with her and came from this relationship, which I will get to a later point, but it just wasn't meant to be.

So, we did the usual High School dating thing, hung out all the time, went to movies and dinners all the time. Introduced her to all my friends, and my family, as well as et her parents. Most of my friends were not really buying into this relationship. They were very skeptical. Most of them kept that to themselves for years. They saw I was happy, and they supported me.

Her parents were divorced, and she lived with a paternal parent and her stepparent. Yet another divorced family in my life. Divorce was becoming a more dominant thing in my life. They told me so many horror stories about the divorce, and how horrible of a person her dad was. Just how much of a loser he was. I never felt right hearing these things. I never met the man, but I could not believe that a person could be that bad. When my ex was not around her mom, she would tell me how she didn't believe the things her mom told her about her dad, and how she just wanted to be around him and talk to him and her stepmom. It was sad to see and hear about it. She wasn't allowed to contact her dad at her mom's house, so my parents allowed her to call her dad when she was hanging out at our house. She would tell how much she hated her stepfather and how abusive he was to her. They would always talk bad about her father and tell her lies about how he didn't want her, things like. She would tell me how her stepdad would put dish soap in her drinks and pour the dirty cat litter box in her bed. She would say how in the middle of a sower he would turn the hot water off. Again, that is what she told me happened at least.

One day after a storm had hit, I was over at their house. Her mom had told me, with such excitement I couldn't help but get excited myself, that God had visited their home during the storm and protected them. She said she knew it was God because of the upside cross that was made from the branches that had fallen from a tree in their backyard.

An upside-down cross? I may not have been a well-educated Christian at the time, but I was sure that an upside-down cross was not a sign from God. There were other stories that they had told me, that I will not go into, which led me to believe that there was something not right about her beliefs. My ex assured me that they were Christians, and went to church here and there, and since that is how I was, I figured all was good.

I never felt right when I would go over there and visit like there was something heavy over there. I always just assumed it was stress, or them judging me for dating their daughter.

Things started moving fast that semester. School was flying by so fast; my relationship was moving fast too. Prom came and went, then graduation was here. It was done, High School was over, summer was here.

Well, let's pause right there and rewind a second. I am being honest and transparent here, right? So of course, we did what all stupid teenagers do, we had sex. She was my first, but I was not hers. I remember that night because it was not what I expected. I figured I did things right and I was going to get told what all the people in the movies got told "oh that was amazing" or something like that. Well to my surprise that is not what happened. Nope, she was quick to compare me to her ex-boyfriends. Size, abilities, what they did better. I mean she did wrap it up with "I mean you should be able to get better at this.". That was nice of her I guess, she had hope, right? What that did for me and to me, well I am sure you can imagine. Yup, it crushed me, to the core. I had something to prove at this point. I mean I had seen enough porn to know what to do right? So, whenever I could, I would have sex with her to see if I got better, and I would ask. Well, I got the answer, not that I wanted, but I got an answer. So, as you can see this relationship became more about proving I was good at it and knew what I was doing.

That summer my parents took us all on a trip. When we came home from a nice relaxing vacation, we were all hit with drama. The drama was not something my parents put up with. But this was drama on steroids, and I had no clue how to deal with it.

I remember that day like it was yesterday. Her mom and stepdad were kicking her out of the house. She had no place to go, so my parents opened their house to her. We all went over to her parents' place to get her stuff so she could move in. They had tossed her clothing out in the front yard. So, we all just grabbed her stuff and took it back to my parents' place. For me, it was cool because I got to spend more time with her. My parents took her into their house and took care of every need she had as if she were their own. They even offered to pay for some college for her if she was interested. She was now family.

I figured if I was going to get married to this girl, I needed to change my goals from acting. I had better get a more reliable career. I started going to college while working, saving as much money as I could to buy a house, pay for a wedding, and get her a car. As things had it, the new career I had chosen was not what was meant to be.

Our engagement apparently caused a lot of drama too. I asked her father for her hand in marriage, and that made her mom and stepdad mad. I guess because I did not go to them, but I always thought one should go to the dad with questions like that.

As a family, we got hit with a big old smack in the face. My dad wasn't feeling well, he never told my brother and me all the details, we just knew that he wasn't feeling well and was seeing a doctor. His doctor went through a gambit of tests and possibilities. AIDS/HIV, Cancer were two of the options that his doctor came up with for the way he was feeling. Clearly, dad was not too happy about AIDS/HIV, not that cancer made him that happy either. Well after all the shock and tests and using my dad like a human pin cushion the doctor finally figured it out. My dad was finally diagnosed with MS or Multiple Sclerosis.

We were happy it was not cancer or AIDS/HIV, but honestly, I was scared. I had no clue what MS was, and what it would do to my dad. I mean was he going to die because of it, was he going to be completely disabled because of it? I had no clue, and the internet was not quite at the stage it is now. Probably a good thing because every time I go on there now to look up issues I either have cancer, I am about to die, or I am pregnant. Around this time is probably the first time I had a serious talk with God. I think it went something like this...

"Umm hey God. I mean Dear Heavenly Father. If you are real, which I think you are, I mean I have been told you are, I need you to take care of my dad. You know stuff, like everything, so you know what he has and what it is. I need you to take it away from him. You can fix everything, so fix this, please. Thanks... In Jesus' name, we pray, Amen."

The medication the doctors put my dad on made him, well in case he is reading this book too I should be nice, so they made him a bit cranky or moody. He started looking into other options besides the regular meds. My nerd of a father was starting to look at alternative medicines, he was turning into a hippy. He started to go see an acupuncturist once a week. He started feeling better and got off the meds. He replaced them with a lot of vitamins and minerals. Now this kind of pissed me off. I had prayed for him, to God, and asked that it just be taken away. Why didn't God heal my dad? Why didn't he do what I asked? I mean come on I was a Christian, I was one of His children and he did not listen to me. But dad was feeling better and he was happy with how he was doing. I wasn't sure why he wasn't mad a God for this, he didn't do anything to deserve this. He was a good man, he prayed, went to church, knew the Bible, all that stuff. He helped people when they needed help, but he now had MS.

For those of you who don't know, MS, or Multiple sclerosis, is a long-lasting disease that can affect your brain, spinal cord, and the optic nerves in your eyes. It can cause problems with vision, balance, muscle control, and other basic body functions. It doesn't affect everyone the same either. If you are interested in learning more about MS or maybe even donate money to a great cause go to the following website.

www.nationalmssociety.org

I think it was a bigger issue for me than it was for him, or my mom even. Since they were good, I guess I had to be good with it. So, I moved on to focusing on other things, mainly myself and my relationship and future.

The week building up to the wedding caused a lot of drama between her and her mom. So much that her mom ended up not coming to the wedding. Something to the effect of if her stepdad could not be there then her mom wouldn't be there. To explain a little, her parents did not get along at all. There was a lot of drama during their divorce and after that, the two of them could not stand to be in the same room with each other. Which made it hard on my ex, as a kid I guess she went through a lot due to her parents' divorce. A lot of separation, and mind games. Negative talk about her dad from her mom, and a lot of lies. That is what I was told, so I can only go by that. I was not there when they got divorced. The thing I found odd was none of my friends had dealt with that stuff when their parents got divorced. I never knew that there could be so much anger, hate, and pain during a divorce.

We got married at a young age, and she shortly after got pregnant. I was going to be a dad. This was not something I had ever thought I would be, let alone get married, but I was good with it. The only issue was I had just quit my retail job. Luckily, she had a good job, but with a baby coming, two car payments, and a mortgage? I needed to get a job, and I needed a job fast. I must give credit where it is due. She helped me find a good job quickly. I was now part of Corporate America. The company was a good one, the pay was not bad either. Plenty of room to grow so I had a path on how to take care of my family.

Our son was born, and I was now a dad. I was going to be the best dad ever. I was going to make good money like my dad, and I was going to do everything perfectly. I was going to learn from the mistakes my dad said he made, and never make a mistake as a father, or a husband. This little baby was perfect in every way. The day he was born I felt the overwhelming joy and happiness, the emotional flood that came over me was scary, amazing, and just totally awesome all at the same time. He was not even an hour old and he was my everything. I couldn't imagine my life without him already.

That happiness was soon replaced with fear and sadness. One day at work I got a call from my ex saying that she was on her way to the children's hospital because there was something wrong with our son, we were still married at this time. I asked her if I needed to leave work now and be with her, she told me to hold off and she would let me know more when she got to the hospital with him.

I will put this here for you, my son was supposed to go see the doctor that following Monday for a checkup, for some reason the doctor wanted to see him earlier than that so he had my ex bring him in a few days' early. Almost like someone or something was watching over this kid.

My co-workers noticed something was wrong with me. One lady I worked with was talking to me during our break and asked me what was going on, so I told her. She said that God would take care of everything. She asked if I had ever accepted Jesus Christ as my Lord and Savior. I gave her my pitch; I am a faith-based person and I believe in God. She said she wanted to pray for me and my son, so I let her. While she was praying for us, I felt something. It was warm, no I did not pee my pants. It was this strong inner warmth and almost a peace. I brushed it off quickly as it just felt good that someone cared about my family.

This same lady prayed for me and with me a lot. She always prayed out loud too, which made me feel weird, to be honest. The only people I thought and had experienced praying out loud were preachers and people saying grace before a meal. She came to me several times asking if I had accepted Jesus as my Lord and Savior until one day on a break she took me outside and to talk about it. I told her I was never baptized, and I never said any specific prayer. She asked me to just repeat this prayer after her, and to say it out loud. So, I complied and mumbled every word she said. When we were done, she hugged me and said that everything would be ok and that God was with me on this.

Every night I would work late to get the overtime and then I would go to the hospital to see my ex and son. One night this guy was in the elevator going down to the café like I was. He asked me why I was there. I told him about our son and what was going on with him. He started to cry, for me and our son. I didn't get why there was so much sorrow in his eyes for me. He said everything would be ok and that the Lord would take care of our son. I asked him why he was there, and what he told me shocked me. He was there to say his goodbyes to his daughter. I think she was about 12 years old and had been in that hospital her entire life on life support. He said that night before getting on the elevator with me he had just signed off on taking her off life support. This man was more upset about our little babies' condition then he was about his situation. The compassion he was showing me was amazing. He told me it was time for his daughter to stop suffering here and to go home to the Lord, and how he knew he would see her again and there would be no more pain. He told me to have faith in the Lord and know that He would take care of our son.

One night she called me from the hospital. She told me that the doctor said it was not looking that good for our son. She said that the doctors could not get him to stabilize with any of the medicine he was on. She told me that the doctor said if we believed in God we should start praying for our son. Admittedly I went to the bottle and started to bury my pain, my anger, and the sadness. The through of losing our son was too much for me to take. Once I was good and drunk, I thought about it. I had prayed a few times in the past and nothing worked, but why not give it another shot. I dropped to knees by the bed and started weeping and praying. Asking God to not take our son from us. To fix him, heal him, just make him better, and to not take him from us. The entire time he was in the hospital I would work late for the overtime, head down to the hospital and spend time with them, then go home and get drunk, then pray.

I remember one night I went to visit her and our son in the hospital. I went to the room and everything seemed to be normal. She was hungry, our son was asleep, she had to pump, I needed food. I told her I was going to go to the cafeteria to grab something to eat. I went to the elevator, and there was a man waiting for it as well. Did the usual "Hello", he said hi back. We got in the elevator in silence.

He said, *"How are you today?"*

"Good and you?" I replied.

"I would have to be you to be doing any better."

"How's that?"

"Why are you here, you have a little brother or sister here?" he asked.

"No, my son."

"How old?"

"Two weeks."

He asked me why, and I told him about Luke's heart condition. He had SVT, no not the Ford the Mustang. He had Supraventricular tachycardia. I explained that it caused my little guy to have an abnormally fast heart rhythm due to improper electrical activity in the upper part of the heart. Basically, we were told it was like his heart was racing at 3-4 times the rate it should. The doctors told us it could be life-threatening for him.

This man that I had never met started to tear up. He said that he was so sorry to hear this. We went to the cafeteria together to grab some food. Before eating he asked if I would mind him praying. Of course, I said not a problem. He prayed for me and my family. He started to tell me why he was there. He said to me that his daughter had been in the hospital for about 9 years now and he just had to pull the plug on her and let her go home to God.

Wait, what? You are sitting here telling me how horrible it is for me and my situation and you just had to pull the plug on your baby girl? WTF?

When we were done eating, he looked at me and said,

"You are a strong young man. You will make it through this. Your son will be fine, and he will grow up to be big and strong just like you. You will be able to make it through everything that comes your way. I see it in you. You are a fighter. You fight the wrong things, but you fight for what is right as well. I can see it in you."

"Thank you, but I am not as strong as you think."

"I don't think this, I know it. God told me. Life will be hard for you, but one day everything is going to come together, and you will be good."

We said our goodbyes. I went back up to the room. What is crazy is while writing this I had almost forgotten that conversation.

Well, we finally got to take him home. We had a little heart monitor for him in case he had another episode while he was home. We would have to cut up his medicine and mix it all up then give it to him. I didn't understand why God did not give me what I wanted. But we had our son back home and it was awesome. I stopped praying, I figured that the doctors were fixing it and I would just do what they said. Giving all the credit to the doctors.

My ex decided that she wanted to be a stay at home, which was a great goal to have. Reverting to what my parents taught me I tried setting up a plan to make this happen. To my surprise she quit her job, a job making a lot more than I did. This made me mad, how were we going to pay the bills and keep this lifestyle up? So, I did what I needed to do. Every day I busted my butt at work, every time the opportunity came up for a promotion, I would go for it. If I didn't get the promotion, I would get told how I must not have tried hard enough. My ex would tell me that I clearly didn't want the promotion, or that I wasn't doing everything I could to get it, that I wasn't working hard enough. So, I started to try harder, and harder. It became an obsession for me to get the raise and promotion. I started to believe that I was not doing enough, that I was being lazy. So, more hours, more time away from my family, more learning so that I could get that promotion.

I am not sure why, but while I was doing this, which is what I thought she wanted, she would also tell me that I was neglecting her and our son. I pointed out how this is what my dad had to do to provide. How he would bust his but all week, then spend tie with the family on the weekends, and that is how he became a millionaire. Like I said earlier in the book, my dad made good money. It just felt like I could never get on the same page as her. She wanted me to get promoted and make more money to support the family, but it seemed like working more to get there was not an option. I was confused about what to do. I started feeling again like nothing I did was right. I stuck to my guns and continued doing what I was doing, and low and behold I got the promotions, I got the raises.

A little bit before our son was a year old, I finally achieved a huge goal of mine. I finally earned my black belt in the martial arts. It was a struggle to get there. I was balancing work, family time, and making time for this dream to come true. She would always tell me she supported me, and I think she did in a lot of things, but when I would go for the things, she said she supported me in, it would be a battle. My parents and I am sure a lot of parents, teach us actions speak louder than words. And I was feeling like her actions did not match up to her words. I am not saying she was a horrible wife at all, I am just stating the things she did and said made me feel a certain way. It was still an awesome achievement, and to have my little buddy with me on the day I got that black belt made it even more special. New goals and dreams started happening. I was going to teach him to be a great martial artist, open a school, and teach with him.

When our son turned a year old his mom took him in for his checkup with his heart doctor. It was an amazing day, the doctor said that the heart issue appeared to have gone away. He was healthy and could get off the medicine. We had no more fear of our son passing away in the night. Now most Christians, and me now, would have given all the glory to God and praised him. Not me, nope, I gave it all to his mom for taking care of him, and the doctors. I totally forgot about my prayers and promises to God that I had made those nights.

So many issues came up from the day we got married. So many signs that maybe we were not good for each other, or maybe we were just not heading down the right path with each other, heck maybe we were not even on the same path at all.

I thought things were great overall. I mean she didn't care if I went to strip clubs, or those restaurants were the girls are barely wearing any clothing, as to protect myself from a lawsuit I will refrain from naming them. I think you know what I am talking about though, you know the place you go to for their wings because they are "so good". What guy wouldn't be happy with a wife that allowed him to go places like that or to strip clubs? I remember one night when she was about seven or eight months pregnant, she told me to just get out of the house, go hang with my friends and go to a strip club. She even called them up and set the whole evening up for me.

Little did I know I was being spoon-fed, or force-fed porn, and I had absolutely no clue what that would do to me, and us. I would go out regularly with her and without her to Strip clubs, we had a couple of Adult magazine subscriptions that we would look at together and even had the channels on TV to go with them. 24/7 porn right at my fingertips. I would come home from work and there would be a magazine on the coffee table for me, or the TV would be on that channel, dinner was being cooked or all ready to go on the table. What a life right? Well not so much. It was ok if she put the magazines out, or turned the channel on, or set the guys night up. But if I did any of that, it was an all-out war, and I would end up on the couch. I would be pissed off, confused, and ready for the fight the next morning. But then I would come home from work, and there it was again on the coffee table, or on the TV.

The magazines were kept in the closet, and I would find myself in the room wanting to go in and grab on a magazine and just drown all the noise in that magazine. But then fear came over me every time. What would she think, what would she do if she caught me? How long would that fight go on for? Sometimes I would walk away and others I would just grab a magazine and zone out. Then there were the times I went into "fight mode" and I would keep us up for hours, to the point where we forgot what we were fighting about. Not my proudest moments in life here people. Every time I dabbled in this "addiction"

I would feel dirty, no pathetic, I would feel disgusting. I would feel all of that all at the same time. I was using those magazines and the TV, and the movies to fill an empty space in my life. I started to expect the magazines to be out, and the TV to be one when I got home. When it wasn't, I would get irritated. I wouldn't say anything to her, but I would just be irritable the enter evening.

At one point I got tired of getting in trouble for looking at them and watching the TV, so I canceled the channel and started to throw the magazines out in the trash. It felt good to get rid of that stuff from the house. But that started a fight as well. Damned if I do, damned if I don't is the way I felt.

Money was always an issue, there were things she wanted to get done or do, and I just could not provide. Medical expenses were killing us, two car payments, credit card bills, everything financially was crashing down on us. I was the only income earner in the house and that put a lot of stress on me. We ended up filing bankruptcy so that we could get ahead again. That was a huge punch the nuts of my man ego. I couldn't provide for my family; I could get them everything they needed and wanted. I spent a lot of time talking down to myself, as well as being talked down to. Now, most of the time her complaints about me were accurate to a point. I mean if I went to a strip club and she got mad about it, she would let me know how it was wrong for me to go to places like that, and that I was wasting money that could go towards bills. I was just confused as to why it was ok if she set it up, but not if I set it up. If I forget to take out the trash, she would let me know that I was lazy and forgot. That is all accurate, but not how I thought a husband and wife should treat each other.

We even did that whole thing where you make a mess and leave it just to see if the other one would finally take care of it. Setting each other up for failure. With all of this, she told me she wanted another kid.

I could barely make the bills as is, and she wanted to have another kid with me? I was lazy, I was stupid, I was worthless, and she wanted to have another kid with me? Well heck, maybe things were not as bad as I thought so sure why not. I mean who would want to be with a guy like me who was so lazy and stupid and unmotivated like I thought she said I was. So, with her wanting to have another kid she must have just been mad at the time and really didn't mean any of it.

Like I said the money was tight, we would sit down and run budgets to see how we could do what all we wanted to do. When things were tight, she would say we need to ask my parents for help financially. I never liked that idea for a few reasons, and I would tell her. One I didn't like borrowing money, she would say I needed to let it go and that my ego was out of control. Two when I asked my parents for money in the past they would tell me no, she would point out how my parents gave my brother money and that if they really loved me and wanted to be fair that they would give me money too. So, after long conversations with her, building me up to go to my parents and point out how they would give my brother money and that I needed help, so they needed to give me money too. Well let's just say the conversations with my parents would go exactly the way I thought, no money was given. I would report back to her about what happened, and I would get told how I didn't try hard enough, or that I didn't say the things she told me. If I had just done and said what she told me to they would have helped. Sometimes it was nicer, and she would just point out how they liked my brother more than me.

Well, that was great because I had spent so many years as a kid thinking that exact something, so it was easy for me to fall back into that same crappy negative self-talk lifestyle. You know the whole "You suck, nobody likes you" blah, blah, blah. I was right back at it, and I had help. Even today I do not think that she did this intentionally, and she may not have even meant to do this. It was hard times for us both, she had goals and dreams, and I did too, we just were not on the page.

We had our second child, got a bigger house, and new cars. Because that is what you do when you don't have the money to pay your bills. We were good at putting on a front like everything was perfect in our relationship. We had stuff, nice stuff, stuff our friends liked. They would say how they wish they could do the things we did and have the things we had. That all fed my ego, I felt like I was the man. I had this stuff, yet I was feeling more and more empty. I would get put down, and I would put her down. I was the king of getting mad and putting holes in the walls, which made me quite the handyman when it came to patchwork. Again, I was no saint, I was not the perfect husband, nor was I the perfect dad I had wanted to be.

But I did a great job of making people think I was. People would tell us all the time "Man you two can never get divorced because if you did it would be a sign that no marriage could ever work." We were hoping for people and their relationships. The magazines started to make their way back into the house. History was starting to repeat itself. It was ok for her to pull them out, but I could not unless I wanted to get into a fight.

The day our son found my "stash" is the day I took every single one and put them in the trash again, and everyone that came in the mail went right into the trash as well. I thought I was over it; they were gone, and I didn't have to deal with that anymore. Then there was the internet. That made it easy, she could show me videos, but the kids couldn't get to it because they were too young and couldn't get on a computer. But again, when I looked by myself, I would get caught and nailed to the wall for it. Eventually, I just became numb to it. I didn't want to look at it, I was desensitized by it. It no longer did anything for me, and I knew if I looked, I would have a huge fight heading my way.

Promotions were coming in, raises were coming in, and money was going out the door faster than I could make it. I had let my wife down, she had to go get a job, and could no longer be the stay at home mom we wanted her to be. I suggested that we sell the purses with the LV on them, and the ones with the little horse-drawn carriage. Also, maybe we needed to stop buying all this name brand stuff. I don't think that was an option because the names brands kept filling up the house, and I never tried to stop it. So, she got a part tie job, then got back into Corporate America. And man, she killed it. What took me five years to obtain, financially at my job, she blew away in about two years. She was amazing at her job. Money wasn't getting better, just more stuff. More fights, more arguments, more emptiness, less happiness.

The numbness started taking over everything in my life. Being around friends, I was numb, drinking... I was numb to it. Nothing made me happy, I didn't talk that much when people were around. I just did enough to appear that I was there and engaged. Besides, when I did talk, she would just talk over me. We were no longer a married couple, but two people who lived in the same house and were raising to awesome kids. I still don't know if she ruined it if I ruined it, or the porn. To make it easy on myself I would love to say it was all because of the "addiction" I had, the fascination I had with pornography. That would be the easy way, outright? Just blame it on something like that and take no ownership at all. All I knew was that was not a marriage. That was not a way to live life, that was not happiness.

When we would fight, one of us would inevitably throw out the word divorce. She would say that it wasn't worth it and she wanted a divorce, she would throw her wedding ring at me. Then there were times where I would take the ring off her finger and tell her to just divorce me seeing as I was so pathetic. The threats of taking the kids away from me would really hit me hard, so a lot of the time I would stop and start begging her to forgive me. I would say it was all my fault and that I would change. I would beg her not to take the kids away from me. It seemed like when I fell in place like that and took ownership of it all, took the blame for everything, then it was good. So, I just took the blame for everything. I even took the blame for our sons' heart condition. That's right I was taking the blame for a medical condition.

Our fights were so bad and started to impact the kids, badly. One day we got into an argument, why sugar coat it, it was a fight. Right in front of the kids in the kitchen, we were fighting about something, something so idiotic, I can't even remember what it was. The point here is not what were we fighting about, but the fact that it was in front of both kids. I was cleaning the dishes and she was making a cup of tea. Our little daughter was in the kitchen playing and being completely adorable as usual. I was told to get our daughter out of the kitchen, well that was it. I had enough of feeling like I was being pushed around. Like the mature adult I was, I told her to do. That went back and forth for a bit until I got pissed. I slammed pot down on the counter whipped around and yelled at my precious little baby girl to get out of the kitchen. Well, she thought I was playing and ran to her mom, bumping her mother in the back of the knee. That sweet spot that makes a person drop. Her mom dropped the pot of boiling hot water on the counter, it shattered. Water went everywhere, all over the kitchen counter, the floor, and my gorgeous little baby girl. All down the right side of her body, all she had on was her diaper.

We grabbed her and got her under cold water as quickly as possible. I can still hear her screams in my head, and I can see the panic of our son's eyes till today. We wrapped her up and I started packing our son up to take our daughter to the hospital, and literally, I started getting yelled at that what I was doing was wrong, and that I couldn't do that to our son, that she would take our daughter to the hospital and I just needed to stay back with our son. I complied again with what I was told to do. That was not the time to fight or assert dominance in my eyes. Little did I know what damage and ammunition that doing this, was about to unleash on me in the future.

As she was pulling out, she said she would call me and keep me posted. I waited by the phone to find out how bad it was. When she finally called me, she said that we would need to meet with a plastic surgeon because they would have to possibly do skin grafts. She then told me that I should have grabbed our daughter when she told me to. If I had just listened to her and done what she had said this would never have happened. This was my fault, and at that time I again took the blame. I told myself over and over that if I had just done what I was told our daughter would not have been hurt. I told myself that I did this to her and that I was horrible for it. Pushing myself further down into the darkness.

I went right to pray for our daughter, asking God to make sure she was ok, and that if she had to have surgery that everything would go perfectly, and no one would ever know that I hurt her. Crazy enough when the time for the checkup came the doctor told us that the burns were healing up perfectly. He said it looked like the burns were weeks old, not days. He asked if we gave her vitamins and my ex said yes. He said we were lucky because that is what was helping the burns heal. Not my prayer, not God, but the vitamins. So again, no credit from me to God for taking care of the problem. I gave all the credit to the medical industry, my ex for doing what she did, and the vitamins. Our beautiful little girl was going to be ok, with no surgery.

For years I beat myself up for that day. I could look at pictures of her with those burns without wanting cry. I would talk to my ex about it and she would continue to agree with me that it was all my fault. I kept opening the door for the accusations. I took the blame for everything, so she blamed me for everything. I can't even be mad at her for that, I asked for it constantly. It got to a point where she started to tell me that I was never there to help with the kids, not even when our son was in the hospital. She convinced me that I never showed up to support her. For years I forget about taking my friends to see her and our son. Like it never happened. It wasn't until later that I started to remember what happened, I will try to explain that later in the book.

Chapter 7

It's All My Fault

Life was really sucking for me by this point. I believed that everything bad that happened in our lives was my fault. I believed that I was never there when people needed me to be. I started believing that my parents didn't want and never did. Nothing was going right in my eyes, and from what I thought. Even the songs I listened to started to seem darker, and angrier and more depressed. Everything around me just seemed dark, sad, lost, and depressing. Happiness stopped living in me and sadness took over. It became the norm for me to take the blame for everything, even if I had nothing to with the situation.

Throughout this time, I started getting this pull, this nudge, to try and find out who God was. I can't really explain it in words if you are still reading this book, I am sure you can tell I am not that great with words. The first thing I did was got a Bible from my parents' house to start reading. I mean why not go to the book about him, right? But I would start reading it and fall right to sleep. Either that or it would not make any sense whatsoever and I would stop reading. I was looking for that huge smack in the face. I would jump around that book like a jackrabbit, from book to book. Confusing myself and getting lost in what I was reading. I tried The King James Version, NIV, motivational Bibles, Student Bibles, and nothing was meaning much to me. I could not connect with anything in there as I did with music. I tried listening to Christian music back then, and that was not working. So, I gave up on it.

I mean why bother? He wasn't listening to me, he wasn't fixing my problems, I didn't feel the presence of God in my life. I just felt emptiness, sadness, and anger.

The fights were getting worse between my ex and me, to the point where I was no longer sleeping in the guest room, or on the couch. I was getting in my car and driving to an empty parking lot and sleeping in my car. Then coming back early in the morning before the kids woke up. Sometimes with coffee, donuts, flowers, or whatever I thought would get me out of trouble. At one point to help me out she wrote me a letter, handwritten. It was a list of everything I did wrong, and what she wanted me to change to stay with me. Nothing about what we could do to fix anything, just all about what I had to do to fix things. It was about 30 pieces of notebook paper, front and back used up completely. It pointed out everything wrong with me, and like I said everything I did wrong. I would read this note, this letter, this map on how to fix my marriage almost daily. I wanted it embedded in my brain what I needed to do to fix my family, my household, and my relationship. Every day, I would read how horrible I was, how lazy I was, how messed up of a person I was, and how much of a loser and a jerk I was.

That letter alone could have been a chapter in this book. But I tortured myself daily reading it. Thinking that it would help me become a better dad, person, and husband. It only pissed me off, hurt my feelings, and crushed me.

I got to a point where I just wanted everything to be done, I didn't know what that meant or looked like. She started to try and help me figure out what was wrong with me, so we went off to the internet. Again, the place that tells me I am pregnant, have cancer, or that I should be dead by now. And honestly one of the sites said I had testicular cancer and that is why I was feeling the way I was. She found some sites that did psychological tests online for free, just answer the questions and boom they tell you what is wrong.

She was nice enough to answer the questions with and for me. It kind of went like this, she would read the question and the answers, then she would say "Oh this one sounds like you, don't you think?" I would just say to click on that answer because she knew best. The diagnosis was depression. I didn't like that, there was no way I was depressed. I took the test several other times and it was more stress-related, but she was sure that I was depressed.

It would come up in conversations, and the more I got told I was depressed and that the issue was depression, not stress, the more I would feel depressed. The more I would buy into the depression excuse, the more I wanted it to end. Then that turned into I wanted something else to end. I started thinking of all the pain I had caused her and the kids, both physically (our daughters burns) and emotionally. She would say things like "You are always saying you want things to end, do you mean you want to kill yourself?" Then those thoughts started to creep in. Maybe that is what I meant, maybe I wanted to end my life? Now I am not saying my ex forced me into depression, nor am I saying she wanted me to kill myself, this is just a series of events that led me down a path.

At one point I started working from home, I thought it would be great because I would be able to be around her and the kids more. With this, I would be there when she needed me, and work would not be able to be the cause of my time away. I was actually working for her. Not sure this was a good thing for either one of us. To be honest, she was fully in control at work, she was my boss. And she was my wife at the time, so you know, happy wife happy life, right? I did what she told me to try and make her happy, but it wasn't working, and I was so far down that dark black hole I couldn't see any light. Nothing I did at work was right, I was accused of taking advantage of her, I was being lazy and not even trying hard enough. Admittedly I hated that job, it was not me.

At this point, I was not fully invested in the depression idea, but if I was depressed like the internet said I clearly had to be thinking of suicide and that is what I had to have been meaning when I said I wanted things to end. I started thinking about what it would be like if I was no longer around. Based on what she was telling me, I came to the conclusion that she would be better off without me. Sadness had fully taken over my thoughts. I started thinking everyone would be better off without me around. I started thinking about how I would do it, pills or just shoot myself? Then I would laugh it off and tell myself "dude you're not depressed. This was truly ridiculous to me.

Well she was convinced, and happy wife happy life, so we went to the doctor and she told the doctor about what she thought it was and why she thought I was depressed. We talked about what the internet said. Using her answers, and the doctor was more than happy to prescribe me an antidepressant. I wanted this to be the fix so bad. I wanted to be back to the happy person I was, the positive person I worked hard to be in High School, the person that people liked.

The first day of taking that prescription I got so sick. I was so drained by the end of the day, but when I got home and she asked how I was doing, I lied. I said it was amazing how good I felt, when, in reality, I felt like crap. I couldn't hold food down at all that day. Things went well for a bit, then we got into an argument, about what? Again, I have no clue. But this was bad, the thoughts that were running through my head were about killing myself. She kicked me out of the room, so I left the house. I know I really didn't help matters that much throwing fit myself and "running away". I needed to go think somewhere. This time was different, this time I had a voice telling me to just grab the gun and end it. So, I grabbed the gun out of the drawer and left the house.

For about two years I did this. I would leave pissed off, upset, crying, thinking I was about to lose everything. I figured why do that, why not just end it now. I would sit in a park, a parking lot, the side of the road gun in hand. Loaded and ready to go. Sometimes even sucking on the barrel, tears running down my face. Part of me telling me to pull the trigger. Everyone would be happier without me. I wouldn't be able to hurt her or the kids anymore. Pity party? Yes. This happened just about every night for 2 years. No, not fights, but suicidal thoughts, leaving the house, sticking a gun in my mouth, wanting to end it. Just wanting to die and get away from everything I was fucking up in my life, and everyone's life. I could go more into this, but I am not trying to make people feel sorry for me. Just showing you all how weak I was, and the stupid thoughts there were flowing through my head.

This other voice screaming at me "DON'T DO IT, JUST PUT IT DOWN". It was loud, almost deafening. Sometimes the voice wasn't there, but music would cause me to not do it.

Remember I was being told how my parents didn't like me as much as they like my brother, well I bought into that fully as well. One night I grabbed the gun after an argument, I went and parked in my parent's driveway. I was going to show them how much pain they caused me. They would wake up and come out to me, dead in the car. This would teach them for making me feel like I was nothing, this would make the regret liking my brother more than me. Sitting there in my car that voice was there again. It was saying not to do it, and that this was not the answer. So, I listened and went to a parking lot to sleep in my car. Then got up and went home with the usual coffee and breakfast. I apologized again and asked her to forgive me.

One day it was the worst, the meds were making me sick every day taking them was a task on its own, thoughts of suicide were definite, vivid, crystal clear. I didn't like it; I thought these things were supposed to make me feel good and happy. That morning I told her I was going to go get an office job. I am not sure if it was how I approached it, and if it was the fact that I pointed out I couldn't work for someone like her, but the insults started flying out of her mouth, and I was not taking it anymore. I fought back, started yelling and screaming at her. I was not pathetic, I was not a loser, I was the man of the house and I demanded some respect and support. I needed her to support me and understand that this kind of job was not for me. Next thing I know I have the gun in her hand, and I was trying to get her to shoot me. Telling her if I am so pathetic and worthless then just pull the trigger. I then tried to do it myself. I had the finger on the trigger, pointed at my head, locked, loaded, and ready to go.

Something came over me, this feeling of power just bulldozed me. I couldn't do it. I couldn't pull the trigger, and I couldn't even keep my hand up. My hand lowered and put unloaded the bullet dropped the clip. The gun was now empty and on the counter. I told her to call my dad, to call someone, I needed help. She called the cops; I called my dad.

Short of it, I had my dad take me a hospital and check me in. I knew in my heart I was not depressed, but I was lashing out and acting like I was. I spent a few days and nights there and was able to clear my mind. I saw people in the group sessions who were a lot worse off than me. Even in the group sessions that I went to daily, the counselors said that it made no sense to them why I was doing those things, that to the I was clearly not depressed. They suggested that I go to counseling, and even said it would be a good idea to go to marriage counseling. Which I did. Instead of dragging that story out I will just say, I thought marriage counseling went well, she thought that there was no need for us to do that. So, we stopped going.

I took myself off the meds and started feeling great again. I started feeling that pull again to connect with God, to start reading the Bible again, and this time the feeling to go church was there. Every church we went to was way too big, or too small. It was too old fashioned and too modern. We couldn't find that" just right" church. She stopped going and I kept searching. During this time, I completely destroyed my relationship with my parents. See my mom never came to visit while I was having my little vacation in the hospital. So, when I got out my ex quickly jumped on that and pointed out how it was wrong of my mom to not come to visit. And of course, I agreed. Not once did I think to ask her why. I just assume my ex was right and it was because my mom didn't care enough about me.

Edward Bowers

I remember telling my dad in a parking lot that I never wanted to see them again, that they were both dead to me. I told him how he needed to get his wife under control, and how horrible they were for how they treated me. I latterly threatened to beat the crap out of my dad if I ever saw him again. I told him I wanted him out of my life for good.

Not too long after that, and making some additions and upgrades to our house, we started looking at moving. The house sold and we were off to a new state. I thought I had hit rock bottom with all of this, but that was not case. We moved away from our friends, and my family, to a state where I knew nobody, and I had no job. She said that this move would be great, a fresh start for us. Away from all the bad influences in our lives, i.e. my family. She assured me things would be better for us. I honestly think that was the intent to make things better. I had my idea of what better looked like, but I am not sure what better looked like to her. I had been church hoping this whole time by myself trying to find a church for us to go to, trying to find a spiritual home for us. I thought I had found one right when all this came up.

So, we moved out of state, closer to her family. We had a huge house to move into that we couldn't afford, we got her a new car, that we really couldn't afford either. A new chapter in life, a new state to live in, new house, new car, same old decisions, same old fights. We were just changing locations, and items, but nothing else. No more church hoping for me, we didn't need the church. We had our fresh new start here in this new state.

Chapter .8

Down Fall

We moved to the deep south, the Peach State, Georgia. I spent the first two months trying to find a job. Applying for jobs left and right, and in this economy, I had to make a full-time job out of looking for a job. I also did some odds and end jobs for the in-laws that lived out here. When I was not looking for a job, I was trying to keep the house tidy and whatnot. There were times when I would be applying for jobs and doing phone interviews so I would not be finished with cleaning or laundry when she finished working. I would get told how I was not trying hard enough and how I was just being lazy, how I didn't want to work and just wanted her to take care of everything. Nothing was changing for me, or for us. We were still getting into fights and arguing like crazy, throwing the word divorce at each other left and right. The relationship was just as toxic here as it was there. One of the agreements was I could work towards opening a gym and martial arts school. Every time I would go looking to do that, it would start a fight. I was even getting mixed signals on this one from several angles. My mother in law was telling me about places that would be great to start one, she even helped me find a place that had a school in it and the owners wanted me to buy it from them. I landed a job, not making much but it was something I enjoyed doing. While I was working here, I continued to pursue the martial arts school. But when I did, my mother in law would tell my ex about it, and that would start a huge fight between the two of us. She said she wanted me to do it, but when I went for it, I was told that it was not the right time. I would be told that it was selfish of me to not focus on making good money for the family.

Now I agree, money was tight, I should have just gone out and grabbed a job that paid well. I should have focused on the here and now for my family, and I was focusing on the future. I cannot fault my ex for wanting security. I just wanted to build something for my family too proud of, and I knew I could do that with this school.

Well, the job I loved only lasted a few months. The arguments about money were getting bad. My lack of financial contribution was constantly being pointed out to me. Again, I was starting to feel useless and worthless, anger was building. This was supposed to be a fresh start and I was trying to make it one. But I went out and found a new job where I was making more money.

The fighting and arguing got so bad she kicked me out of the bedroom, permanently. She told me she wanted a divorce, that she couldn't take it anymore. She said that everything I had put her through had finally taken its toll on her. A few weeks of living in the guest room and she told me I needed to move out. I had nowhere to go, but she said I would figure it out. She said I was causing too much stress on the kids and the house. I had met a guy who let me move in with him. I still had that long letter on me that I told you about earlier. So, I started reading it again and trying again to do the things in it, to fix my marriage. It was like a checklist for me, start buying flowers more often. So, I did, and I left them on the front porch of the house. Like I good boy I did my chores. The list said to be more romantic, I am horrible at this. It just does not come naturally for me to be like Romeo and Juliet, or Jack and Rose from Titanic. But I took some notes so to speak from friends, and on the dreaded valentine's day, I did what I could. Balloons, flowers, candies, all brought to the house and set up inside before she got home. It worked I guess because she said shortly after that I could move back in.

After that, she started smoking again. I picked up the habit as well, I figured I could spend time with her this way instead of her being outside and me being inside, she also told me it helped her relieve stress. Well, I knew I was stressed so this should kill two birds with one stone. It was one cigarette here, one there, nothing to worry about. I even found another job with her family making even more money, so three jobs in my first year here. It was manual labor which is something I never shied away from. It was actually a lot of fun, and the money was really good. It felt great being part of a family-owned business. The issue was I started smoking very regularly. I went from the occasional smoke to about two and a half to three packs a day. Sorry, mom and dad. The odd thing was I hated smoking, I hated when people would smoke around me as a kid, I wouldn't date a smoker in high school, my one grandma smoked and I hated the way it smelled, the fact that we could not just go do things because she would have to stop for a smoke. Yet here I was smoking like a chimney.

I was also giving into everything again. She wanted something I gave in and we got it. She said to do this or that, I would do this or that. I was doing everything on my checklist, jumping when I was told to jump. If I am being completely honest here, which I am, I was not happy doing it. It's not like I just did it, I would grumble, I would complain. I would argue about things and try to put my foot down. I can honestly say that I put her through hell trying to fix the relationship. I could not become the person she wanted me to be, but I tried and tried. I was like the little engine that couldn't, yes, I know it is the Little Engine That Could, but for me, it was more... I think I can, I think I can.... Nope, I can't. It was strange she told me I had to go find a new job, she didn't want me working for her family anymore. I say this was strange because she had pressed e so hard to work for them several months prior and really sold me on the idea that it would be better for us.

Needless to say, as the fighting and arguing grew, she was done again. I was getting kicked out of the house again. This time was different, not only did she have her family come over to tell me to get out, but it felt different. I could tell she was done and had been for a long time. I knew divorce would be hard, and all I wanted was to be able to see my kids. I had heard the stories from her parents, and her, about how it all went down with their divorce. She promised ours would be nothing like that.

So, there I was going back to that buddy and asking if I could move back in with him. I had no family there, I had a few friends, but that was it. I didn't just move out like that. I fought, I told her she could be the one to move out if she was done. I even said I would move into the basement. I said that I would not be moving out of our house. She even said that if I didn't, she would call the cops. Well, the kids didn't need to see their dad taken away by the police, and I know how most situations like that end up. Even if I was doing nothing legally wrong, I would be taken away. So, I packed my stuff and left. Trust me it was not easy.

I didn't really get to see the kids that much because we were working on all the details of the divorce. I didn't get to see them on Halloween that year, which really sucked because it is one of my favorite holidays. There was no legal visitation for me, so I really had no leg to stand on regarding any kind of withholding of the kids. I also didn't want to make this any harder than it already was. I also did not get to see them on Thanksgiving, yet another one of my favorite holidays. She took them on an awesome little vacation. I tried calling them but there was no cell reception, so that sucked too.

When I did get to see them, I felt complete. Having those two around me is amazing. We would watch cartoons and movies. Go to the park every so often, or just go on walks. They would tell me stories about school and what they had learned that week. Now while my visitation was not in writing so it was whenever it was cool with my ex, I would see them, I was already paying child support. I got over the anger there, because that money was for the kids and they needed to not be impacted by this situation. Their life needed to stay as normal as possible.

One week, I think when I realized that the marriage was over, done, never going to get fixed. I called my parents. Now I had not talked to them in about 2 years at this point. They had not seen or heard from their grandkids because of me and what I said and did that one day in the parking lot. But I felt something telling me to call them and tell them what was going on. That was one of the hardest calls to ever make. I remember I was in my room at my buddy's house. I was shaking in fear, what if I get rejected? What if they hang up on me? What if they don't want to hear from me or the kids? What if, what if? Even thoughts of what if their number changed or they moved? What if I can't get in touch with them? All these thoughts and all this fear ran through my head for three hours before I could get the strength to pick up the phone and call them. It was like that phone weighed a thousand pounds. I started to dial the number, well more like go to the stored numbers in my phone, but I think you get the picture.

I got my dad when I called. Thank God I got him. I could talk to dad and he would talk to mom and all be would be good. I would not have to talk to my mom and hear from her the pain and agony I had caused her. My plan was working out perfectly. I told him what was going on, and that I was getting divorced. I apologized to him for what I had said and done to him and mom. I said to him that I would understand completely if he did not accept my apology I would understand completely. I said I just wanted them to be able to talk to the kids and see them when I had them. He told me he accepted my apology, and he would love to be able to talk to me and the kids. He said how it was great to hear from me, he had missed me and still loved me. He forgave me for what happened back then and was ready to have a relationship with me again. Then the dreaded words come out of his mouth. The words I did not want to hear at that moment, the words that were causing me a lot of stress, my hands were sweating. The words were.

" Well kiddo, let me get mom on the phone because you need to talk to her. I cannot tell her for you, this is something you need to do."

I could have died right then and there. My biggest fear at that moment was talking to my mom. I had no clue what she would say, no clue how hurt or mad she was with me. It seemed like it took an hour for him to get my mom on the phone, in reality, it was like ten seconds. She was on the phone with me, and I said the same thing to her I said to my dad. There was a pause on her end of the phone. Then she started talking to me. My mom didn't pull her punches at all, she never did. She let me have it, she let me know exactly how she felt about what I did. I said to her that I deserved that and I was calling to see if she would like to have me call them when I had the kids so they could talk to the three of us, or if she wanted it could be just the kids. She asked me when I had the kids next and it was that weekend. She said to me...

"This coming weekend? Well, I can't wait to talk to the three of you then. I love you sweetheart; I will talk to you then."

They had both forgiven me and welcomed me back into their home and hearts. This reminds me of the story Jesus told about the Prodigal Son in Luke 15:11-32. I guess some call it The Parable of the Lost Son. Either way, it doesn't matter to me what you call it, as long as you read it. What this reminds me of is the love the Father had for his to where when the son came back home, the father welcomed him home with open arms. No questions asked, he just showered the son in his love. I know there is more to the story, but that part just rings through my head when I talk about my parents and this situation.

So, I made it a point to always call my parents when the kids were with me. They loved it, the kids and my parents. I was working on fixing relationships that I had destroyed in prior years. I was asking for forgiveness a lot. I started church hopping again, trying to find where I would fit in. I heard people talk about God calling them certain places, so I was trying to see where He wanted me because I was not hearing anything. I had been asked so many times in the past had I found Jesus, I figured I needed to find him.

It was very interesting I even went to a few churches with me soon to be ex-sister-in-law and her husband.

I actually had a great relationship with my ex-in-laws during the first part of the divorce. They were very supportive. We would talk about things, never really bringing up the past, just talking about how things were going. They were a great support system at the beginning. They were honest with me if I was doing something wrong, or if my ex was doing something wrong in their eyes. There were times when they would tell me they hadn't talked to the kids in a while, so I would make sure to set up calls or visits when I had them so they could talk to their aunts and uncles. Not that my ex was keeping the kids from them, that I know of, more just making things as normal as possible for everyone. There was no reason in my eyes that the kids extended family should not be able to see or talk to the kids when they were with me.

The church hoping was not going as well as I thought. I was not feeling anything when at these churches. When I would talk to people, I would start feeling judged at some of the churches. Others were so big I was like a grain of salt in a silo. Nothing felt like home for me. But this time I was not going to let anything stop me from finding my church, this was not like the last few times I went church hoping. I was on a mission to get my life right, and I was going to succeed or die trying. I was looking for that church that made me feel peace like I did when I went to church camp with Cory. I wanted that feeling again so bad.

One day my ex hit me up to sign the paperwork. We had divided everything up. I got my truck, some stuff, and my visitation. Every other weekend, pick up from school, drop off Sunday night. I tried to get more time, but I had no place for the kids because I was living with a buddy. And I couldn't afford a place at that point because I was paying out a lot in child support. I was stuck, I couldn't fight anything, I couldn't afford a lawyer, and I didn't want this to get dirty. When I would push back on anything I would get told how if I didn't just sign the papers, she would take me to court and have me slapped with supervised visitation. Phrases like "don't push me there..." and "I will do whatever it takes to stop you from..." would be thrown at e left and right. Should would point out how to me all the time how I was making this hard on the kids, or she would tell me that she is being nice to me by allowing me to have the amount of time with the kids that she was. Well, I was trying to get to a point where I could move on. Also, I was constantly told that the kids were better with her was getting to me, I started thinking maybe that was the case. I mean everything a was reading said dads only got every other weekend. It is what it is, live with it. Like I said I couldn't afford a lawyer, heck I was eating gas station food, or cup o noddle every other day so I had money to do things with the kids on the weekend. One night she said if I just sign this now, she would allow me more time with the kids when I got back on my feet. She pointed out that if I took this to court no judge would allow me to have the kids the amount of time she allowed because I did not have a suitable place to live. I believed her, so I signed the paperwork. I ended up having to pay over half my paycheck to her. Any time I went to get the kids for their time with me, she would ask me about the child support check, regardless if it was due that day, or the following Wednesday. The kids would always be in clothing that was too small, worn out, had holes in them. I would take them to the park and do as much as I could that was free because I was broke, I was making good money, but I was broke. I couldn't buy them new clothing, or new shoes. They would tell me they had some good clothing and shoes, but that these were the clothes they were "allowed" to bring with them to my place. I felt like a horrible dad.

They would tell me about how their mom was leaving them with her parents so she could go out on dates. It hurt a little to hear this stuff. I was giving her child support, she had a great job and made really good money. I couldn't figure out why the kids never had new clothing, and why their shoes had holes in them, yet every time I saw their mom she would have new clothing, even showed me the new gun she had bought for household protection since I no longer lived there. She would text me or call me telling me how she would never be with another man, but was thinking about dating women, then turn around and tell me about how this guy she went out with was awesome and paid for this fancy meal then tried to have sex with her, or that they had sex. She would tell me, not the gory details, but enough to let me know she was having a good time, and that her life was better without me. It was crazy, I didn't need to hear this nor did I want to hear this information.

Now when the kids were not with me, I would chill at home with my roommate, or we would go hang out at a bar. Either way, we were drinking, and smoking about a pack, or two, a night. Trying pathetically to flirt with the girls behind the bar, and unfortunately putting myself back in the types of places where the waitresses are barely wearing any clothing. I was slipping backward and didn't even know it. My daily routine was going to work, come home, go to the bar or eat dinner at the house, drink and smoke, go to sleep (or maybe pass out), repeat. What a life, right?

During this time, I was only allowed to see our son on his birthday for about an hour, before she told me that I was making it hard on the kids being there, and I was making our friends feel uncomfortable. The funny thing was our son was playing with his friends and kept coming in to tell me he loved me and was happy I was there to celebrate his birthday with me. I did not get to see them that year for Thanksgiving because she wanted to take them on a trip with some of her family. She said she would have them call me every night to talk or I could call them. Every night I called, the phone would ring and then go to voicemail, and my texts would go unanswered. I got told there was no reception during their trip, and that it was not that big of a deal, that I needed to learn to just relax. I was invited over to see the kids Christmas morning. Again, after about an hour I was asked to leave because I was again, I was making it hard on the kids just being there.

I had made up my mind that I would not be getting into any more relationships. Throughout high school, I couldn't keep one longer than two weeks, and my first attempt at marriage was a failure. I clearly was not the relationship kind of guy; I was not dating material nor was I marriage material. I was damaged goods now, and I had baggage so I figured no one would be interested anyway. I would just mainly focus on the kids and me. That was my plan and I was sticking to it.

Chapter 9

Falling in Love

The paperwork was signed and had been submitted to the courts, and we were waiting on the signed paperwork from the courts. The day I signed the papers is the day I finally took my wedding ring off. I kept it on even though I knew my marriage was over I wore it out of respect for the fact that I was still legally married. Once it was signed, I figured why should I keep doing this, it is over. Now it was time to move forward.

Again, I wanted nothing to do with relationships. Relationships as in the long term, one person, engagement, or marriage. The last thing I wanted was to get married again. I just wanted to focus on me and the kids. That was my plan, that is what I wanted. I started to talk to a few women here and there, trying to see what would happen, trying to be a "player".

One day my roommate and I were talking about when I used to be a personal trainer. He said he wanted to start paying me to train him and help him get into better shape. He worked out at a nice gym, as a matter of fact, I had worked there when I first moved to this area as a personal trainer. We started talking about what it was like being a trainer up, and who all I worked with. He started telling me that some of them still worked there. I hit this one girl up that I was kind of friends with, I hadn't talked to here since I left the gym, but we were friends on social media. I remember they would give people a one-week membership for free, so I reached out to her to see if I could get a week pass.

We started talking and just catching up. So, I don't have to keep calling her, "she" or "her" I could call her the most amazing women on this plant, my blessing, my gift from God himself. But I will just call her by her amazing name, Bri so that you all can feel like she is a person and not a fictional character that I am making up. Through that conversation, I mentioned I was getting divorced. At one-point Bri sent me some scripture that had helped her get through a bad relationship, Bri said she had never been married, but she felt it would help me as it helped her.

Psalm 147:3 – "He heals the brokenhearted
and binds up their wounds."

Joshua 1:9 – "Have I not commanded you?
Be strong and courageous. Do not be afraid:
do not be discouraged, for the Lord your God
will be with you wherever you go."

*John 16:33 – "I have told you these things, so
that in me you may have peace. In this
world, you will have trouble. But take heart?
I have overcome the world."*

I have no clue what version these are from, I think the NIV (New International Version).

To be honest, I never read them (as a matter of fact I just now while writing this down finally looked at the scripture she sent me), I told Bir I had read the verses when I went up to the gym to pick up my free pass, but I never did. Speaking of that, so yeah, I went up to the gym to pick up the free pass that she had for me. My mission was to get a free pass and say hello to a friend, that was my plan. Side note here, if you have not noticed I have pointed out what "my plan" has been several times here and I hope you noticed that "my plan" never seemed to work. Something else always seemed to happen. So back to the story... my plan was to go to the gym say hello to Bri, grab a free pass she had for me, then go home and chill out. I got up to the gym at about 9:00 PM, I saw a few people that I knew from when I worked there and said hi to them. I ended up talking to Bri for about two hours. Her shift had ended, and we were walking to our cars. We had earlier talked about how hungry we were, so I tried to capitalize on that opportunity to be able to talk to her longer, so I asked if I could buy her something to eat. Yes, that is how pathetic I am, it was eleven o'clock at night I was trying to take her out to eat. She quickly declined. She was nice, she said maybe another time. I asked for her number so we could try to get together another time.... She gave it to me.

I had gotten numbers from other women before, but for some reason, this felt different. It was not a moment of "Oh yeah I got her number…" or "alright another one for the little black book…", I didn't even have a little black book. When she gave me her number, I felt warm, I felt comfortable, I felt accepted by someone, I was feeling alive. I was almost on a high on my drive home. We started talking and texting a lot, I never texted so much in my life. I couldn't believe it; I was getting into a relationship again. This was not my plan, this was not what I wanted, I was damaged goods, I had baggage… What was I thinking, heck what was SHE thinking?

One evening Bri and I were sitting out on the back patio talking and I got a call from my son. He had been given a cell phone by this point so that he and his sister could call me if they wanted, and they could call their mom when they got home from school if their mom was not home. She worked from home most of the time, but sometimes she would have to go out to do some work. Anyway, I get this call from my son. He was crying, and it was very hard to understand what he was saying at first. He was calling because he and his sister missed me. He was terrified that his mom would catch him calling me and that he would get in trouble. He told me that he and his sister wanted more time with me, they missed me. I finally got him to calm down. It was very difficult to hear my little guy crying like that. The pain in his voice was so apparent, even Bri could hear it.

This wasn't the first time one of the kids had told me they wanted to be able to spend more time with me then they currently could. The kids had always been very open with me. These types of calls happened almost every other night. One of the kids crying uncontrollably and begging me to come to get them, telling me all they want is to see me. I remember several times crying myself to sleep because I missed them. I had been involved in their lives every day for several years, and now I was a part-time influence.

I never got told how they were doing at school, or if they were sick, never got told about doctor's visits, nothing. It was like I didn't exist. The only time I was contacted by my ex was when she wanted to make sure that I was paying child support, or she wanted to point out my life must be great and hers was hard and difficult and it was not fair. I felt like I was her emotional punching bag. Now if the kids were bad, you better believe I was getting called, and I would get the whole rundown of what happened and how I needed to fix it because they were not listening to her. I would get on the phone and chew the kids out, they would say sorry, then boom the phone connection would die. I was no longer needed.

I would call the kids every evening, as I was only allowed to talk to them once a day, so I would call to see how their day was and tell them goodnight. I would get told that I am calling too much, but when I didn't call the kids would get told it was because I was too busy for them, or that I didn't care, or I had more important things to do than to call them. It was sad to hear about these things being said to the kids, it hurt seeing the pain in their eyes when they would ask me if I didn't care about them anymore and if that is why I didn't call. All this hurt started to build up inside of me, but I had to push it down so the two kids didn't see it.

I remember several times my ex would tell me that she wished she had it as easy as me, you know being out "partying" and having a life. It was "so hard" on her because she had to be mom 24/7 and had no time like me to have a personal life and get to go out and meet new people or date. Like the jerk I was I pointed out that she wanted the divorce and she wanted the kids the majority of the time so that was not my problem and not my fault. At one point I did suggest that we change the schedule up to give her more time to go out and meet people, odd because I had already had conversations with her about some of her dates from before the paperwork being signed. She wanted to have time to go out, I wanted more time with the kids. It was a win, win situation I thought. She would point out that she needed the child support to pay her bills, and that even if we did a 50/50 split, she would need child support.

The kids had been begging her to allow them more time with me as the missed me, I was begging her to allow me more time with the kids as well because I missed them. She was telling me that she wanted more time for herself. I didn't understand why we could not do this, why did it always have to come down to money.

Eventually, she agreed to shared parenting and equal time for her and me with the kids. I was able to get my own place to live. No more roommate, my own place, I could afford to eat more than just cup o' noddle's every other day. It looked like things were looking up for the kids and me. She told the kids that she was agreeing to more time with me, she told them that she knew it was the best thing for them to be able to spend time with. She told them how she remembered not being able to see her dad when her parents got divorced, and that she didn't want them hurt the same way her mom had hurt her. When we talked about it she told me that she didn't want our divorce to be ugly and militias like her parents. She promised no more changes, and no child support would ever be passed between the two of us and how this change was what was truly best for the kids. They needed their dad more in their life, and I agreed that they needed both of us equally. Lots of promises about how this was it, nothing would change, we could all move on, etc. A very pretty picture was painted.

I found a place quickly, it only two bedrooms, one bath, with a sunroom. It was a start; I could save from there and get a bigger place later. It was close to the kids' school, not far from work for me so again another win, win situation I thought. Oddly enough my ex moved into the same area, with the exact same living arrangements. The kids thought it was strange that their mom moved so close, I told them that it was awesome for them because their mom was within walking distance to them when they were with me. I also said it was cool because the two places were the exact same floor plan so everything would be in the same place as they never really had to leave their home. May not have been the best plan, but I was trying to make them feel comfortable with everything.

The kids welcomed Bri into their lives with open arms and open hearts. Before she came into our lives I would joke with the kids and ask them how to date someone, because I had no clue it had been so long. They gave me rules for dating as well as pointers on what a date is.

The Rules of Dad Dating (according to the kids)

- *No dating anyone taller than you dad (according to my son, that would just be odd if I was shorter than the woman I was dating).*
- *No taking a girl (or woman) to Wendy's. Wendy's is not fancy enough for a date.*
- *She must be able to drink beer. If she is not old enough to do that, then she is too young for you dad.*
- *Chinese buffet is not for dates.*
- *Be nice and say nice things to her, girls don't like mean people.*
- *Open Doors for her, girls like that.*
- *She must be pretty.*
- *Pizza Buffet is not for dates, well not for adult dates.*
- *Remember to talk to her dad, girls like being talked to.*
- *Make sure you pay for everything dad; women should not have to pay for a guy.*
- *Make sure she is nice and likes kids so that you can introduce her to us.*
- *And remember dad, no buffets for dates.*

NAILED IT!!!! That's all I can say there.

So, when the kids were with me things were great, Bri would come by and hang out with us or she would even spend time with just the kids. Then there were times when she would respect the fact that the kids and I just wanted to be together, just the three of us.

I remember our first date like it was yesterday. I picked her up from work that night. I had been out of the "game" for years and had no clue what I was doing. It was like I was back in high school. I had a single long stem rose, red, on the front seat of my truck waiting for her to open the door and see it. Good lord, she looked so damn amazing, vibrant and happy. Almost glowing with a light that could get rid of any and all darkness in the world, including my heart. So, we went to this place right around the corner from where I was living at the time. She had Salmon for dinner, don't as why I remember that I just do. In the middle of dinner, my son called me. I asked if it was cool if I took the call told her who it was and she yes. After dinner, I asked if she wanted to go back to my place. We went back and sat at the counter and had a glass of wine. I just remember how beautiful she was. All I wanted to do was kiss her. Her eyes glowed, she sat there in that chair with so much confidence and perfection. We just talked and laughed about stupid things. My heart was racing the entire time like I was a 14-year-old boy. I was already head over heels for this woman. I finally got the balls to look her in her eyes, and just to let you know her eyes are like looking into heaven, by the way, I asked her *"Would it be inappropriate to kiss you right now?"*.

My heart was racing, what if she said no? What if she thought I was a tool for asking that on the first date? What if she thought I was a pig for asking? What was I doing? I had no clue what the hell I was doing? She said no it would not be. It was like in the movies. I scooted closer to her, and she came closer to me. Her eyes were already closed, mine started closing. It was all in slow motion, closer and closer I got to her. Then, BOOM, lips connected. I was warm all over, from head to toe. Then I reached out with my hand and place it on her arms, moved up to her shoulders. Her hands went right to my face holding the side of my face. This first kiss was surely Heaven on earth. I took her back to work a little later so she could get to her car and go home. The ride home for me was amazing, to just sit there and play the entire evening back in my head over, and over again.

From there we were like teenagers, texting each other most of the day and all night. I remember I would not eat throughout the week, so I had money to take her out, as well as have money to take my kids out when I had them. Just about every night we would get together and I would buy her Starbucks or Chic-fil-a. I had no money so I would not eat, just so I could spend time with her. All-day at work I thought of her, everywhere I looked there was something that reminded me of her. We would go to parks and walk around or go to Barns and Noble and just look at books and magazines. Some of the best dates of my life. I loved watching her look at all the bridal magazines.

I must admit that I was heading towards love with Bri in a very short amount of time. I wanted to move slower, but not love. I told myself I was in love with her about a week into dating her. I remember the night I told her, and no I did not come out and I say it. We were sitting in my truck out in front of her best friend's house. I told her "I think I am falling for you."

She said, *"what do you mean?"*

I said, *"Bri, I think I am falling in love with you."*

I didn't think, I knew I was in love with her. The deepest love I had ever felt in my life. The strongest, emotional love. Man, I was freaking out. What the hell was I doing to this amazing woman? I was a failure, I was older than her, I had so much baggage. But she told me she loved me too. Fuck! I was done. I was in love with Bri. I was going to do right this time. I was going to make it all work perfectly. I went home and was feeling so high from this moment I didn't go to sleep. I think I finally slept after about two days. But I was madly, deeply, in love with her.

I remember we would send each other songs to listen to that reminded us of each other. She sent me country songs, pop songs, she got me listening to music that I never listened to before. Me? Well, I sent her heavy metal. Well, the first song I sent her was a song by Korn called "My Wall" because the lyrics described her and what she was doing to me perfectly.

And along came something sacred
I never knew what I found

The demons dance around, elated
They're hurting me

I put my wall up each day
You tear it down
I hide in my space
The space you found
And one of these days
I'll come unbound
The feelings I hate
Will finally drown

Falling awake in a nightmare
Images of horror abound
Thought I stumbled upon salvation
Hell I found

I put my wall up each day
You tear it down
I hide in my space
The space you found
And one of these days
I'll come unbound
The feelings I hate
Will finally drown

Well, I'll never be the same
It's the greatest lie ever told
No, I'll never be the same
I sold my soul

I put my wall up each day
You tear it down
I hide in my space

The space you found
And one of these days
I'll come unbound
The feelings I hate
Will finally drown

The chorus "I put my wall up each day, you tear it down, I hide in my space, the space you found" She found me in my darkest moments of life, and any walls I had up would come crumbling down with just a smile from her.

I tried to keep open lines of communication with my ex-in-laws for the kids' sake. When talking to the kids they would ask if they could talk to aunt so and so, or uncle so and so. I wanted the kids to stay in contact with all their family so I would make it happen, phone calls, Skype. I would do whatever it took for them to be able to see and talk to their family, regardless of if they were on "my side" or "her side". I would hear from her family that they never get to see or talk to the kids when they were with her, her being my ex. So, like I said I made it happen. I noticed that her family would start telling the kids *"Now don't tell your mom we talked, last time we talked your mom found out and I got in trouble. We need to keep this a secret."*

I too was getting "in trouble" for the kids talking or seeing her side of the family when the kids were with me. My ex would tell me all the time "that is my family, stop trying to be in my life...". I thought I was doing right by the kids and her family by letting them be involved in each other's lives. Her family was claiming they hadn't heard from or seen the kids in a while, the kids wanted to talk to them and see them, so I made it happen. The kids were not divorced from anyone, their mother and I were divorced from each other. That should never have affected them like this. I did what I could to make things as normal for them as possible. Admittedly I still allowed the phone calls, visits, and Skype to happen so that the kids could see and talk to their family members. I figured I could put up with being yelled at for the kids, as long as the kids got to be involved with all their family members. Looking back, I see that I probably should not have allowed this.

Every time I would turn around a new bill was coming in from when I was married. A new debt that I was not aware of. Or my ex would tell me the kids needed something for school and I needed to pay half. No child support being exchanged, but somehow, someway I was still having to give her money for things. Even with that I thought things were good, had my own place, got to see the kids half the year so I was very involved with them and their upbringing. The job was going well, I was starting to dig myself out of that financial hole called debt, and I had a beautiful woman in my life that my kids really connected well with. One-night Bri and I were watching TV, the kids were in bed asleep, and I heard a sound outside, and saw flashing lights through the window. It was the repo man, there to take my car away. I didn't realize how far past due I was, it was a bit of a struggle to get all my payment information from my ex after the divorce. I knew what address to send my payments to, but no clue what was owed. Well, it appears that a lot more was owed than I thought. I am not saying this is my ex's fault, by all means,

I should have gotten my info sooner and looking back there were other ways of getting that info.

The next morning Bri came over to help me get the kids to school and helped me find a new car. I was humiliated because of this. My ex found out and she hit up her sister to see if they had a car I could borrow until I got a new car. I was shocked, but thankful, for the help. Shocked because I had been getting my butt chewed for "being involved" with her family, thankful that she helped by reaching out to a family member of hers who was willing to help me out for a little while. I found a new car, just a little clunker, to get me around. Next thing I know my ex shows up in a nice new coupe. She had gotten rid of her other car and got something nice, sporty, and fast. She played it off like she was close by and wanted to check on me to see if I was doing ok, then started to downplay how nice her car was. Now I am not saying that she was intentionally rubbing it in my face, but at that time I took it as if she was. My ego was way out of place, and it was bruised up, so I took things personally that I should not have.

Things started to get bad between the kids and their mom. My ex and my son would get into arguments a lot, over things like he didn't clean his room. These arguments would turn into all-out screaming matches between the two of them. Then the next thing he knows he is getting told: *"well if you don't like it then just leave, go live with your father."* A few times she would text or call me and tell me I needed to get him to do what she told him to. I would try my best over the phone to calm him down and get him to go clean his room or do whatever it was his mother asked him to. This started happening with our daughter too. They would get into arguments over how our daughter didn't like how her mom treated her big brother, things would blow up, then I was on the phone having to defuse the situation.

One night I got called and told I needed to come to get our son out of her place. She said she was "done with him", I could hear him crying in the background. She said that it was *"time he lived with me more because he was of an age where he needed to be around his dad more."* While we were talking, she told me that she knew this was the case because her mom had to kick her little brother out a few times to go live with their dad at this age. She said this right in front of our son. I ended up going and picking him up to come to stay with me. The sad thing for me was our daughter was there watching all of this godown. I remember her being very upset. As my son and I were walking away I remember my ex telling our daughter that it will be ok, that her big brother was not healthy for the two of them, and that he needed to go away for a while.

The weekends I would get our daughter I remember her telling me how her mom would tell her that her older brother was bad, and not healthy for her to be around. She would get told things like *"your brother is a bully..."* or how *"your brother is just like your dad and likes to be mean to girls...".* Our daughter would tell me that her mom was always telling her bad things about me and her brother. She would tell me that her mom would tell her things like *"we don't need them, or men like them in our life."* I was shocked, how could you tell your ten-year-old daughter these types of things?

This went on for two months, all the time my ex would be calling me telling me how much she missed her baby boy. How all she wanted was for him to come back home to her. During this two-month time frame, I worked with our son trying to get him to understand that he was just a kid and that he just needed to understand that his mom loved him, and only wanted what was best for him and his sister. He started to show signs of missing his mom, so I suggested that maybe he should go back to see his mom. Not because I didn't want him around, but because I felt as though he needed to spend time with his mom to rebuild the relationship that was so badly damaged. He agreed and said that he wanted to try and fix things with his mom. So, I set it up, and she took him back in.

Well, that lasted about two months, before she started to get on him about everything. She would insult me in front of the kids, and when they would stand up for me, she would punish them. Our son started standing up to his mom, and she was not having it. Calling me every night, telling me half the story, then expecting me to just side with her. I admittedly would not just side with her. I would ask for the details of what happened, and why people reacted the way they did. I would point out how the kids' reactions were not ok, and that they needed to obey their mom, and that when at their mothers' house it was her rules. Repeatedly I would tell them to show their mother respect and to show her the same respect that they showed me. That was a mistake, so to speak because then my ex started to ask why they respected me more than they respected her. She determined that the reason the kids respected me was that I "had no rules" and that "I was their friend, not their father". This was the story that she later used against me when the custody battle went into a full-blown war. But that is coming soon, I don't want to get ahead of myself here.

So, she ended up one night kicking our son out again, this time I get the call from our son, crying his head off. He said "dad I got into a fight again with mom. She said that she doesn't care where I go, but I am not allowed to be here at her house anymore." I tried to calm them both down, and figure out what really happened, tried to solve the issue. But again, my ex said that our son just clearly needed more of a man's influence and that he needed to be with his father more. Again, stating that she knew this because she had seen this type of stuff happen in her family before with her parents and her younger brother. It seemed like a lot of history repeating itself.

I went that night and I picked up our son along with his belongings. The next night I get a call from my ex telling me that she was calling the police on our son and me because he took his bicycle that she had given him for Christmas. She said if one of us gave the bike back in the next 24 hours she would drop the charges, but if I did not comply with her demands I would end up in jail. And yes, she told our son that if he did not bring the bike back to her, she would have me arrested. Over the next few years, she would threaten to call the police on me for withholding the kids, etc.

If I recall this happened on a Thursday or Friday evening. The following Monday while I am at work, I get a text from my ex asking me to call her, so I did. On this phone call, she said that our daughter wanted to move in with me. According to my ex, our daughter did not want to end up in a position where she got kicked out by her mother as her older brother did. I said I did not think this was a good idea, that it was allowing the kids to set the tone, and it allowed them to be empowered. Well, as usual, my ex disagreed with me. She advised that she knew this type of thing would happen because this is the kind of stuff that happened in her family when her parents got divorced. At the end of the conversation, we agreed that our daughter would move in with me.

As the weeks went on the kids started opening up to more of the stories their mother told them about me. She even went as far as telling the kids that I was cheating on my girlfriend, and that she was cheating on me as well. She told the kids that one day while surfing the web, or as she called it 'The World Wide Web", that she ran across an advertisement for a dating site. And that one this advertisement there was a picture of my girlfriend in her underwear. So out of complete curiosity, for the well-being of me, she just had to click on this ad. Low and behold, by clicking on this advertisement it took their mom into my girlfriends' apparent dating profile. She told our kids that their future stepmom had an active account on a dating website. These types of lies about me cheating on her and cheating on my girlfriend were told to the kids almost daily. It's the same kind of thing her mom and dad did to her and her brother and sister when they were younger.

Things were going better for the kids living with me. Their grades started going up, they started to rebuild their relationship with each other. The kids were with me and at this point saw their mom every other weekend. She gave me a couple of hundred bucks a month to help with them, a far cry from the eleven hundred dollars a month I was paying her while living in a friend's extra room, but hey, for me it was not about the money. It was about the kids being happy, getting good grades, and having a relationship with each other. Things were going well.

Chapter 10

Finding Christ

One thing I remembered hearing throughout my life, or mainly childhood, from a bunch of people that seemed to have their stuff together, was that during the rough patches in their life they would just lean into God, or that they would just lay it at the Cross. Now I knew what they were saying, but I really had no clue what they were saying. What I did know is that they had something going on in their life that I did not, and they attributed it all to God. So, what was going on between them and God, that was not going on between God and me? What I did know is that I needed to do something, anything, to get things to calm down and get on the right track. We started going to church, funny how that all went down. So, prior to my ex kicking our son out of her house, she had started going to a little church just down the road from the apartment community with both lived in. I remember one of Bri's friends invited us to her baptism on Easter Sunday that year. The kids were with their mom this weekend, so Bri and I went to her friends' church, I mean it was Easter Sunday, and that was one of my usual days to go to church. That and Christmas Eve. No offense if you are reading this and you only go to the church those two days, I mean hey you gotta start somewhere, right?

So Bri and I went to church with her friend. That Monday when the kids came home, we did the usual talk. You know "how was your weekend?", "What did you guys do?", all that. Well, when it came time for me to answer I told them how we went to see Bri's friend get baptized at her church. You would have thought I told the kids we went to Disney without them. My son literally got mad at me. When I asked the kids, what was wrong they were very quick to express their disappointment in me for going to church without them. They made me promise to take them to church the following Sunday, and it had to be this church that their mom took them to. Like a good dad, I said ok.

Admittedly, I went to the internet to look at this church and see what it was all about. I did not exactly trust my ex to pick a good church for the kids. Seeing as every time I found a church to go to while we were still married she would find something wrong with it, regardless of how much the kids and I loved it, that is if I could even get her to go to a church. Anyway, I could not find anything about this church. But I had already made my mind up that this was not going to be a good church, and that we would not be going back to it ever again. See at that point in my life I had no clue what God was capable of, I had no clue who He was.

The weekend rolled around finally, and the kids were excited to take me to their church. Saturday evening when the kids were in bed, I told Bri that I was not going to like this church and that there was no way my ex could find a good church. I said that we would go once just to make the kids happy, then we would go find a good church to start going to.

Sunday morning had arrived; it was time to keep my word. We all packed into the car, we made a stop at the Quick Trip to grab something to eat and a Monster Energy Drink. Now I am an early riser, so we were headed to the first service, 9:30 I think it was. We pull into the parking lot; I start feeling nervous. The thought of going into this church was starting to freak me out. I still to this day cannot explain this strange feeling I was experiencing. As a matter of fact, I don't think I ever told anyone about that. So, if you are the first person to read this book you are the first to find out about this. Well except for the person who did the proofreading, but I think you get the point? So, I was feeling nervous, shaking a little bit.

We walk into the church, people start saying hi to us and introducing themselves to us. A few of the recognized the kids from the time they were there with their mom. So now I am telling myself, "ok man now they know you are divorced, here comes the judgment. It was going to be ok because I was ready for it, bring on the judgment". Even the pastor came up to me and introduced himself. He recognized the kids, and by this time their mom and some of her family members showed up. The Pastor asked me if they were my kids because Bri did not look like the lady the kids came with last weekend. I explained I was their dad, and that Bri was my girlfriend, then I pointed at my ex and said, that she was the kid's mom and my ex-wife. He looked at me and said "Oh wow, that is awesome. You know divorce happens, but the fact that you two come to the same church during the same service is really awesome." I was beyond confused at this point; this church was supposed to be the same as all the other churches I had gone to and hated because I felt judged. I remember walking into the sanctuary for worship and seeing the worship leader on stage. Every guy on that stage had tattoos, big mountain man bears, and then there was the worship leader with a mohawk. Yup, no need to go back and re-read that. He had a mohawk, and no I am not talking about a Mr. T and Chuck Liddell style mohawk, I mean an actual mohawk.

Now when I had gone to church in the past, even in recent times, the music was very church music. Slow, gospel type music. This place was playing music that sounded like the stuff I would listen to on the radio, just about Jesus and God, instead of sex, drugs, and rock and roll. One song they played was called Oceans. This song brought me to tears, I literally was standing there singing this song while fighting back tears. Well, I lost the fight if you wanted to know. Tears rolling down my face, trembling, but not feeling sad. It was an overwhelming feeling like someone understood the pain I was going through, and that there was some sort of hope for me and my kids. I felt welcomed like I was home. How could that be, I was supposed to hate this church. It was supposed to be some sort of snake worshipping church that was led by a bunch of freaks. I was not supposed to feel comforted or welcomed. I remember between the worship and the sermon they had a lady go and up and do announcements. She said, "we know it is not by chance that you are here... we are so glad you are here.". It felt like she was saying that the kids, Bri and myself.

After service was over, we all got into the car and started to talk about the service and what Bri, and I thought about. I couldn't find anything bad to say. I tried to come up with something that I did not like about the church, the worship music, the sermon, something, but I could not for the life of me find something wrong with it. Like I said at that point in my life I had no clue what God could do. I had no clue what he was doing in my life or with my life. The kids asked if we would be going back, and both Bri and I said yes. We even started going to the church on the weekends I did not have the kids.

I quickly became very attached to the church; I did not know why but I wanted to get involved. I wanted to get to understand God more, and the church more, I even started wanting to serve. I was jumping into this pool with both feet, no dipping the toes in. I wanted peace, I wanted a better life, and I was not going to stop till I found it. The more involved I got, the drama my ex caused me. To the point of telling me that it was her church and I needed to stop going to it. One day she told me it wasn't fair that I was making friends at her church, that they were her friends. Eventually, she left the church, which was not my intent. I thought it was doing good for the kids to see their mom and dad being able to be in the same building, and what a better building than a church, for us all to have been in and not argue or fight. She would tell the kids that the church was a cult, and she would tell me that I am not doing right by the kids by taking them to a cult and that one day she would report me for endangering the kids.

I found out after she left the church that she had been telling people in the church that I cheated on her and that is why she divorced me. But when I started coming and getting to know people, and they started to see the type of person I was, these people who once believed her stories about me stopped.

The more I drew closer to Him, the more my life started getting turned upside down. Things started to get super crazy after I got saved. On the day of my baptism my son looked at me and said: "Dad, I need to get baptized today." He told me that while he was listening to the Pastor talk, he felt God tell him that he needed to get baptized. I made him go call his mom and see if she would come down to see him get baptized. She told him no, and that he needed to wait to get baptized so she could plan a party for him for getting baptized. He did not want a big production made of it, he just wanted to get baptized and that there was no reason for a party. She was mad at him for this but told him fine.

After that things went well for a couple of years, I mean a few issues here and there with the kids not wanting to talk to their mom, or them being rude to their mom on the phone when they felt as though their mom was attacking me or their future stepmom. So yeah at this point we were talking about marriage. I even let my ex know about this choice as I thought she should know about a person who was going to be that involved in her kid's life. She told me she wanted to get to know my girlfriend a little bit better as she was going to be the stepmom of our kids. I was thinking sure what could possibly go wrong here. I thought maybe this would be a good thing, and that we will all be able to work together raising the kids. Boy oh boy was I wrong. Bri comes back from having coffee with my ex one night, and boy was she on fire when she came home.

See it appears that Bri had to spend about four hours listening to my ex-wife talk about our marriage, and everything that was wrong with me. According to my ex, she just wanted to warn Bri about me. She also felt as though she needed to warn Bri about how she needed to get used to me needing multiple partners, because "One woman was not enough for me." Bri had to listen to my ex tell her how "awesome" of a dad I was and person, but out of the other side of my ex's mouth she had to hear about how I was a horrible person and I needed several partners in the bedroom. Not sure where that came from as it was not the truth.

Luckily for me, even with what my ex-wife told her, Bri still said yes. That's right, I in a roundabout way, asked her to marry me, and she said yes. Looking back, I should have done it the right way, the traditional way. But not me, no way, I mess things up thinking I am funny. She had told me about a dream she had where I proposed with a huge stone in a ring, she said yes, then I took the ring away laughing saying I was joking. Even in her head back then I was a jerk. So, when we got home, I took the ring out, slipped it on her finger and said, *"Well is that as big as the one in your dream?"*. She was shocked, all she could do was look at the ring.

I said, *"What do you say?"*

She said, *"What do you mean? You didn't ask me anything?"*

I said, *"Bri, will you marry me and my two kids?"*

She said, *"Yes!"*

Then this is where I messed up because that's what I do. I proceeded to say, *"Round two, ding, ding."*. She had told me several times in the past that my first was just practice. So, I thought in my selfish, stupidity, and childish sense of humor thought she would find that funny. I am so sorry Bri! So incredibly sorry.

Kids were excited, my parents were excited, she was excited, and yes... I was excited too. Her parents were not exactly happy about this announcement, and to be honest I can understand why. I mean looking at everything that you have seen so far in this book, it is not like I had my stuff together. I was divorced, with two kids, not planning on having any more kids, living in an apartment, a bit over ten years older than their daughter, so yeah I can see why they were not jumping for joy when they heard we were getting married. Don't worry ladies, I may not have dropped to one knee when I proposed to her, but I did talk to her dad beforehand.

The engagement ring, well it was not the stereotypical diamond solitaire ring. I am not that normal. The ring was a tanzanite center stone, with a couple of smaller diamonds on the side of the center stone. I tell you this because within a day or so of Bri posting pictures of the ring on social media I get a call. This was an odd call from my ex. She was first complaining about the kids, then about my parenting style, then she congratulated me on the engagement, after insulting me as a husband. From there she proceeds to tell me "Well I hope you got her a real ring; I mean like I hope you did go cheap and get her some stupid colored stone for her ring. She is young and I am sure wanted a real engagement ring, don't rob her of that. I mean I liked the ring you got me, but it was never a real ring... It was a colored stone." For the record, I got my ex a "promise ring" when we were in high school and it was a blue colored stone. The engagement ring was, in fact, a diamond solitaire with two rubies, one on each side of the center stone.

See this was how just about every call would go between the two of us. Complain about the kids, tell me I am not a good dad, and that I am not being a good ex-husband. Then go into how I need to be a better husband to Bri than I was to her. These types of things would get under my skin, make me mad, and put me on the defense. All of this would then turn the phone call into a full-blown war, thus ruining the remainder of my day. No matter how much a tried, I would end up getting mad, no pissed off. I was finding it very difficult to even answer the phone when she called because I knew it would start with insults, then I would get pissed, then I would eventually turn the call into a fight. This pattern went on for years. I would try and keep the conversations limited to text, but she would get under my skin with the insults. I tried emails, same thing, insult after insult, after insult. Then I would fire back. Once I would break and start firing back at her, she would point out how I had better stop or I would regret it, she would tell me that she would have the kids taken away from me. She would point out that She could easily get the kids taken away from me.

After a while, she started telling me how I was turning the kids against her, and that the only reason the kids "did not like her" was that I was trying to replace her with Bri. She would tell the kids that she knew what I was doing and that one day they would see that she was not the "bad guy" and that they would see who the "true bad guy really is". She would tell them how her mom was convinced her younger sister to hate their blood father, so with that, she knew what to do to turn kids against their parents, therefore she could tell the kids that could tell that I was trying to turn them against her.

These things went on for about 5 years. Constantly telling the kids that Bri and I were trying to brainwash them to hate her. Constantly threatening me with the police, or that she would take me to court and take the kids away from me forever. Telling me how she was being nice to me by allowing me to have time with the kids. It was very difficult to deal with all of this. Hearing from the kids about all the lies they were being told. Always being told that I was a horrible father by talking to a church that she felt was a cult.

She would tell me that her uncle was a church leader, so she knew what a cult was. She would also tell me how her dad was a cop, in another country by the way, and so with that, she knew what laws I was breaking, and she also knew ways to have the kids taken away from me. She would do the same to the kids. This caused so much stress on the house. Kids were fearful that they would be taken away from me forever, or at least until they were adults.

Finally, I had enough, I needed to find some peace, I needed to be free from these threats. I had been praying about this situation. First, I was praying that God would just make it stop. And if he would just make it stop, I would do A, B, and C. That's right I was wheeling and dealing with God. Like that ever worked for anyone. Just to save some time, because I feel like I am taking up a lot of your time with all this information, my prayer life was all over the place. I was hearing about people praying and healing themselves, or others. Praying about an issue then hearing from God and getting the answers or direction. I heard people tell me that they challenged God in their prayer, and things got better. So, I was praying every which way I could, it was more like throwing mud at the wall and seeing what sticks. If I might suggest something to you, this does not work, praying like God is a genie in a lamp and here to grant you your three wishes is not the way it works. Treating Him like fire insurance isn't the way to go either. But I am sure you already knew about that.

Chapter 11

A New Blessing, Another Struggle

So, I want to be honest here again with you, today is December 30th, 2019. I stopped writing this book for about 2 years. Something told me to stop, that something was going to happen here that I needed to put in this book. I had no clue when I stopped writing it what was happening or going to happen. So, prior to writing this chapter let's see what has happened?

Bri and I got married, and it was the most amazing day of my life. I felt whole again. I felt complete, loved like everything was going to be ok. I had Bri the love of my life, the kids loved her, she was perfect for us. I could write a book about our wedding alone. One of the most amazing things about this wedding besides the promise to spend the rest of my life with this amazing woman, this amazing blessing from God himself to me, was how she walked down the aisle to Korn. Damn, that's right gents, I had the perfect wife. Her hair was perfect that day, her smile, her dress, all perfect. Oh, the future looked so amazing and bright for me. God damn, she was and still is the most beautiful and amazing woman on this planet.

Let's see, we got married, we moved out of the apartment, we got a nice rental home. I felt like I had a reason to live, and that reason was my family that God was blessing me with. I had hope, I had a vision, I had clarity in things. Smooth sailing for me. Man, it would be amazing to tell you all this was the end of the book and everything was amazing and perfect from here on out. I wish I could leave you with some sort of amazing message on how you need to not give up and never lose hope, trust in God and everything will turn out perfectly. While there is a lot of truth to that, I have to say that there is more to this story from here.

But alas, that is not the case.

One Friday evening I come home from work, the kids and Bri were sitting there waiting for me to get home so we could go grab dinner. Bri was acting odd. She said she was going to go get ready for dinner. Now I must say this. When Bri said she was getting ready it's not like we had to wait hours on end. Nope not at all, this girl got ready in a flash. This time she was taking a long time. The kids told me she was acting strange, not like herself. So, I went up to the room. There was my beautiful bride on the bed.

I said, "Hey babe, what's up?"

She had a little box in front of her, I went to the side of the bed and repeated myself. She politely tossed the box over to me. I was thinking shit, what have I missed, it's not her birthday or mine, and not our anniversary? What am I missing? I opened the box. I was going to be a dad again. That's right it was a pregnancy test showing that we were going to have a baby. We had agreed on no kids, but here we were. Expecting! I kind of tossed the box back at her. I went silent.

"Oh, God... Are you for real? Are you kidding me? I am messing my other two kids up. Are you giving me another child? How? Why? I can't do this. I am old, I am broke God!"

I sat on the floor in the middle of the room I went silent for about 30 minutes. Thinking of how am I going to do this? Planning and planning, running numbers in my head, we only had three rooms, where will this kid sleep? I got up, I said, "Well we need to tell the kids."

I heard her crying a little bit. I asked her what was wrong, and I will never forget her words.

"Eddie, I don't want you to think I am trying to trap you. "

"Bri I would never think that there is nothing to cry about."

She kept crying.

" Bri why are you crying?"

She said *I am going to get fat."*

I couldn't help it, but I started to laugh. I told her she would not be getting fat that she was pregnant. She wanted to know why I wanted to tell the kids so early. So, I told her that she has been acting odd recently and I felt that the kids should know why. So, we went down to the kids and sat them down and told them the amazing news. The kids were so excited, they both asked if they could pick the name. Bri and I agreed that they could pick a name and we would go with it.

Luke picked "Landon Allen Bowers", and Sydney picked "Harper Nicole Bowers". Bri and fell in love with both names and never looked back. The kids were so excited they came up with the names within minutes of being told about a new baby coming into our lives. Man, life was looking amazing, Luke wanted a little brother, and Sydney wanted a little sister. When we told the kids Luke said, "Well that explains it." Bri and I asked what he was talking about, he said "Well Bri has been being really mean recently, so her being pregnant explains it. It's going to be a boy." Ugh, kids, am I right?

Bri posted updates on her pregnancy on Facebook every week, and good lord she looked amazing every day, every week, every moment. The most amazingly beautiful pregnant woman God ever created. I had it made it, I'm just saying, Life was amazing.

But wait...

My ex. The kids. The courts. That's right, next thing I know, the emails and phone calls start flying. Once the posts started about Bri and I expecting a baby, my ex started her shit back up. Accusing me of parental alienation now. She accused Bri and me of brainwashing the kids and having a kid to keep the kids from her. I mean it wasn't enough that she accused Bri of legally changing her middle name to match Sydney's. No, clearly that was not low enough. Nor was telling the kids that Bri and I were dating each other while my ex and I were still married. Because that is healthy. So, during Bri's entire pregnancy we were fighting a battle with my ex. Little dude was born, emergency c-section. I almost lost my baby, and almost lost my bride. But God saved them, and he saved them for me.

Oh wait, you guys might want to know, or not... We found out that we were having a boy. Luke wanted to know as soon as we found out, Sydney wanted surprised. So, we told Luke, and with Sydney we got her ear pierced a second time with a blue gemstone for "it's a boy!!!". This little girl was so excited to have a baby brother coming. Again, God was blessing us all with happiness, and amazing things.

Let me just say right here and now that Bri did not get fat. She was pregnant, and she was the most amazingly beautiful pregnant woman in the world. Always glowing. She was the perfect pregnant wife a man could ask for. She was all about the social media posts and updates on her weekly changes. Even today I see the posts on the "memories" and she looks more amazing now than she did then. How did I miss that back then? She knew this was a blessing, she showed little fear, just rays of happiness and joy.

Here is another perfect example of how I don't deal with things properly. As if you have not figured that all out by now. On the day of her baby shower, I had a church security training thing to go to. That's right I was the head of security, I felt special being that. Not the right feeling to have, not humble at all. That Saturday was the last day of the training and she had the baby shower going on. Her mom set it all up, did an amazing job decorating and whatnot. Towards the end of the training, I started getting texts from friends at the shower that Bri was not happy. As a matter of fact, she was upset, and she needed me there. My wife needed me there. I went and got my oldest and we headed to the shower. When I got there, I went up to her and hugged her, I was already mad. She was upset for sure, she started telling me what was happening and all that did was fuel the fire.

Why was I mad? Because what I was being told was that Bri was upset by the actions of her mom and dad. How the baby shower was not going as she had wanted it to, and all this was stressing her out. I went into defense mode, well maybe more like fight mode. I think I was looking for a fight at this point.

As people were leaving, Bri was getting more and more emotional and upset. She was starting to argue with her parents. She was feeling attacked by them for not showing appreciation for what they had done. We were cleaning up and I said something like "do you want me to take care of this?". She said yes. It was like hearing the bell ring, time to fight. I heard her mom say something to her and all I heard was Bri say "I did thank you, and I do appreciate what you did for me." I went off, pointed out how there is no need to keep bringing this up because Bri had already said thank you and whatnot. Ended up following her dad outside arguing with him. I remember telling him that I understand they put a lot of effort into this for us, and we have said thank you and told them how beautiful it was, but if that was not good enough for them then I was sorry. I also told him that if they continued to act this way towards my wife, we would no longer be involving them in things like this. I told him they were acting like children because I was acting like such an adult at this moment. When I got back into the building Bri was having it out with her mom. I told Bri to just go to the car and I would take care of it. I remember telling, not asking, but telling her mom to drop it and to stop upsetting my wife. I was informed that Bri was her daughter and I could not tell her what to do or how to talk with her daughter. My response was simple "Bri is MY wife, MINE! Not yours anymore!" like Bri was a piece of property. Like she was something I owned, not a person, not my partner, but property. I had no right to talk to them like nor did I have the right to treat her like property.

Bri went in on a Friday for a checkup. Well, it appears that our little dude, our blessing was about 2 weeks from joining us, but hadn't grown in about 2 weeks. So, they sent Bri to the Hospital to be admitted. Our little was coming early. I get a call from Bri that Friday morning letting me. She told me how he had not been growing for about 2 weeks. I was like *"Oh God, come on. First, I almost lost Luke to his heart condition as a newborn. Then Sydney with her burns."* I calmed down and remembered that God healed Luke and his heart condition, and Sydney has no scars from her burns. I thought to myself *"Gods got this Eddie, everything is going to be great, you're going to be a dad again.".* Left work, raced to the hospital to be with my bride. I think she got checked in at 11:00 AM that Friday. Well, Friday night came, no baby. Saturday, no baby. We watched the UFC fights on the TV. That's right, perfect wife right there.

The heart rate monitor was not my friend that weekend. Littles' heart rate was all over the place. Bri was uncomfortable. Saturday evening was rough. The doctors tried to get Bri to push a little bit, she was in pain. I remember her looking at my crying, tears coming down her cheeks. She said she couldn't do it. I told her, yes, she could, she was strong and could do anything. She had no choice, and she could do this. I told her I was there with her and we could do this. Sunday morning came around, still no little dude. I knew something was wrong. The heart rate monitor being all over the place. Plus, I hear the nurses talking about c-section. At one point I heard them say *"We need to get a room ASAP for her, or the baby and mom could be in danger."*. That's right, emergency c-section. At one point I remember going outside to get some fresh air and starting to break down, weeping and crying in the parking garage. I was just praying that God would not bring this much joy into our lives just to have it taken away. I had lost so much already.

Well, some good news here, everything went fine, our beautiful little blessing, Landon Allen Bowers, was born healthy and screaming his little head off. Like my first two kids, I was the first to hold him. I knew right then and there that God was blessing the crap out of us. When we got to the room the kids got to come in and see him first. Sydney burst into tears; she was in love with him the second she saw him. Luke didn't want to stop holding him. Family and friends flooded the room. I was running from the hospital to the house to take care of the kids and be with Bri. I brought the kids to see her and Landon every day. We brought Landon home, slept on the sleeper sofa because we transformed the dining room into his room, and Bri couldn't really go up the stairs. We traded shifts getting up with little, but for the most part, Bri took care of him. She was a warrior, still is.

After she healed up and I went back to work, the custody situation started to ramp up a bit more with my ex. Started going to co-parenting sessions, kids were put into counseling. The battle was starting to get bad. One night after counseling I came home without the kids. The counselors felt as though I should not see the kids for a month. I got home and Bri was sitting there with little in her arms. The look on her face when the kids did not follow me was terrifying. Tears started coming down her face. I had to tell her that we would not be seeing them for a month. This broke her heart. My heart was getting crushed again by my ex. The accusations and threats were too much. The thought of not being able to see my older two kids became too much for me to handle. I had to go back to stuffing my emotions deep down so I could function. Little did I know I had so much baggage stuffed down below that there was no room for these new emotions.

That was one of the longest months of my life, and I think Bri's as well. She was hurting as much if not more than me. She stepped up when the kid's mom abandoned them. But we had little dude to focus on. Bri and I prayed, her more than me. My heart started getting hardened. Not good gents... Don't do this to your wife or your family.

After the month of not seeing the kids ended and the kids could start visiting us again, it was great. My family was complete again. All five of us living together again. The house was full of love and joy again. Struggles come, of course, visitation schedules suck. We also needed a bigger place so the kids could have their own rooms and whatnot. We found a new place and moved again. Moving on upright? Well, the custody battle took another ugly turn. About 6 months in the new house, the kids got taken away again. I was being told I would never get to see them again. The costs were building up. It was like my ex was doing everything she could to ruin me financially.

One night I got a text from my dad saying that he and my mom wanted to skype with Bri and I. It was strange because my dad almost never hit me up for this, normally it was mom and Bri and I hit them up. But sure, we loved skyping with my parents. Little did I know I was about to get hit with some of the worse news ever. The second we got the video working and I saw my mom I knew something was wrong. They started off with "We need to tell you, kids, something." At first, I was like "Oh fuck, please God don't tell me they are getting divorced." Shit that would have been a cakewalk compared to what they told me next. Mom had cancer, stage 4 colon cancer. Bri held it together, she had dealt with cancer in a family member before. Not me, that was my mom. Dad had MS and I was ready and prepared for me to go, not my mom.

Sorry dad, but I had many years to prepare for you leaving us, but not my mom. So yeah now I am dealing with that, plus I had to tell my kids.

So, the next weekend I had the kids I sat them down with Bri, and we explained that we were going to Skype with Grandma and Papa, but Grandma my not have much energy to stay on for a long time. I had to explain that Grandma had cancer to my kids. Thank God I had Bri there with me as a support system. They took it well, sad of course. They asked if this meant Grandma was going to die. I did what any great father would do, I told them no. I told them how strong my mom was and how she was going to fuck cancer up and beat it. Man, I almost believed myself when I told them. A couple of weekends later the kids were back over and talking to us about how they let it slip that Grandma had cancer to their mom. Wouldn't you know it, but my ex told them that it was fake. This coming from the woman whose mom would claim she had cancer like a million times just to get the family together for the holidays.

If things were not bad enough my depression started rearing its ugly little head again. But wait... I wasn't depressed, I had everything I wanted, this was just a little setback. Nope, not my dramatic ass. That depression just started kicking me in the nuts over, and over again. I just tried to hide it through, when I should have been open and honest with my wife about it. How? I had God in me. Damn, I should have talked about it and gotten help then. But no, not me, not the guy who had it all together. I just went back to old habits of stuffing it all below, deep down inside me.

Still battling for custody of the kids at this point. My ex started bringing in more people that needed money to work the case. She was really pushing for that parental alienation claim. Now she was claiming that she was going to take the kids away from me for good. Bri and I knew we could not afford to keep fighting the battle and keep the house. We had to act fast. We found a friend that would allow us to move in with them and pay a lot less in rent so we could afford to pay the attorney fees, mediation, and all that shit.

One day both of my kids pulled me aside separately and told me the exact same things. They told me that they could not handle seeing me working so hard and fighting so hard for them. They noticed it was ripping me apart. They both told me in their own words that they wanted me to stop fighting for them. That they wanted Bri and me to be happy, so they asked me to give up on the custody battle. I talked to Bri about it all and we agreed it was time to throw the towel in. It was ripping us both apart emotionally. So, the next mediation meeting I had I just signed off on new paperwork. Limiting my time with my two older babies. Back to seeing the older two every other weekend, living in the converted one-car garage of a friend.

I will admit at this point in my life I did not care what happened to my ex. I just never wanted to see her face or hear her voice ever again. There was so much rage, even after I signed off on what she wanted she was pissed. The original paperwork she had her people send to the mediation room had my paying out so much child support and back child support there would have been no way for me to live and take care of Bri and our little dude. But I honestly was just thinking "fuck it, send me to jail for not paying, then I will have no income and she will get nothing from me.", but my attorney would not let me sign that paperwork. She sent back changes and I ended up signing off on it. Well, some of you might be thinking *"So you just gave up?"*. You are right, I had to make a choice. Run Bri and I into the ground fighting this claim, or just sign and start taking care of Bri and out little dude. So yes, I tapped out, I choose Bri and Landon over the older two kids. Please don't think it was easy for me. I felt like I had failed Bri and the kids, as well as our little dude. So much guilt, anger, and pain.

I thought maybe, by signing off on all this crap my ex would view that as a win and leave the hell alone. Nope, wrong again. I guess that she felt as though this gave her the right and power to treat me like a child and as if she had control over me.

By this time, it has been long enough for moms' doctors to allow her to travel even with her port installed. She came out to visit us. God, it was good being around my mom. When I was at work Bri and my mom would take Little Dude out and have with him. It was August right around my birthday and hers. We had to take it easy, due to her cancer, she would get tired easily. She would tell us how she was going to be fine and it was shrinking, she was going to beat it. God, I wanted her to be telling me the truth so damn bad. I could tell she knew something, was hiding the truth from us. But hey, I was with her and she was with us. She went back home to Texas, and not too long after that Bri and I had a falling out with the lady we were living with at the time.

Bri and I started feeling unwelcome at the house, so we started looking around for somewhere else to live. We found another friend who wanted us to get into a healthier living arrangement and they offered to have us live at their place till we got back on our feet. Well, the night we accepted the offer. Yup you guessed it, the lady got pissed off at us and right as Bri was putting little dude to sleep, she kicked us out of her house. Thank God we had friends who dropped what they were doing, and they came and helped us get all our stuff out of this ladies' place. We took it all to her parents' place.

I never did what it took to have a good relationship with her family. I know another area I messed up. So, guys if you are reading this and are in a relationship, make sure you treat her family right.

They accepted us with open arms. I remember that night a cried in my mother-in-laws' arms telling her I was so sorry that I was failing as a son-in-law and husband. She told me it was ok, her dad and mom told me that people go through rough times.

Chapter 12

Another Move

A couple of days later Bri and I moved into the other friends' house. They set up the game room for the older two kids. We had a room for us, and Little Dude had his crib in the closet. This was a blessing, but felt like a swift kick to the nuts, the ego, my "manhood". My wife was upset about this and there was nothing I could do to fix it. I was failing as a "man", a husband, a father.

Now, not then, I see where I fucked up a lot with my relationship, oh and don't get me wrong I am not saying this is where it started. Looking back, I see a lot of areas where I fell short and really fucked her up and our relationship up. Not to mention the damage I did to my older two kids. So, let's keep rolling through this shit storm I have created and continued to create. Oh yes, that's right there is more. And no this is not a pity party; this is me seeing the areas I messed up and fell short. This is taking ownership, yes, I know it takes two, but I can only take ownership of my mistakes. Pointing fingers does no good, trust me on this one. I have spent a lot of time pointing them.

She had some feelings about things then and I would "listen", but then tell her we just needed to hang in there and hunker down. Everything would get better and we would be back to having our own place, and all would be good.

Great problem-solving skills right? This has been an issue for me for a long time. Never realized it till later. I thought I was great at it. Bri would always tell me "Eddie you are better at fixing things and solving problems than me." Little did we know I just swept the problems under the rug.

Several months later, Bri was feeling down and out about things, looking back I cannot blame her at all. Just some butting of heads with our friend, feeling like she was being belittled, things like that. Back then I was like "deal with it we need a place to live". I know real love and concern being shown there, right?

Another friend of ours had space in their place, like a little 2-bedroom apartment, that they were willing to rent to us. It would give us a room, and little dude his own room. We would not feel like we were living in some one's house, but maybe feel like we were in our own place.

We jumped on the opportunity to feel like we had our own place. We spent about 4 hours in total packing and moving into the new place. Now I am not sure that I did this all properly, that's for sure. I worked long hours, then add traffic, so the last few weeks at the prior friends' place I would get up early, head to work then come home and head right to the room. Take care of things I needed to, come out to eat dinner, then Bri and I would head back to the room and take of things we needed. Spend time with each other and little dude. This made our friends feel like we were unappreciative of them helping us.

That Christmas a friend of mine was talking to me, he knew one of my dreams was to open a martial arts school and gym one day. He asked me what it would take to open one up the way I wanted? We started talking about it, and he said to just write some info up and get it to him with pricing within the next week. Over the next few days, I created a spreadsheet with everything I would need for just a martial arts school, just a gym, and a combination of both. Sent it over to him. The next day we met up, he said to me that he wanted to fund the project to get it opened.

I started picking up clients for personal training as well as one on one self-defense clients. Staying late after work to train people at the gym in the office, as well as spending my weekends driving to people's homes to train their kids. I made some extra money, started feeling like I could do this. I took up a lot of time that I should have been giving to my wife, but I told myself that I was doing this all for her and the family. Little did I know I was being super selfish, just focusing on me and what I wanted. At least the way I was doing it that is. Bri and I started planning it all out, the equipment we would buy, how we would run it together. She spent days and hours going out looking at spots that would work for the gym. She would send me pictures and info on every location. She amazed me every day at how focused and determined she was to help me get this dream of mine up and running.

The feeling of having our own space was amazing. Little had his own room, we had ours. A kitchen, living room, etc. Shortly after we moved in my ex determined that it would be best if our oldest son lived with me. Again. Bri and I made the changes to this small space to make it so he could live with us. What the hell were we doing, no paperwork again? But we loved him so much, he was in so much pain emotionally, how could we reject him?

He moved in with us, and my baby girl visited every other weekend. The family was coming back together again. Things seemed to be doing good, in my eyes that is. There were times that he would stay up all night playing games on his computer, talking to his friends. Bri would get upset because of how loud he was, I would too. I would ask him to keep it down, tell him to stop being so loud, remind him that little dude was in the next room sleeping. This was just about an every night occurrence it seemed. Bri and I would get into small arguments about this type of thing. Admittedly I did not handle the situations well with my wife or my kids. I will get more into that in a bit.

Bri and I would Skype with my mom and dad weekly so that they could see the kids and watch little dude grow up. We would get updates on my mom and how she is doing. She looked tired, happy, but tired. The kids would be so happy knowing we would be talking to them. As time went on the

Skype calls would get shorter and shorter. She just didn't have the energy to stay online for hours like she used to.

We found a spot to open the gym, started setting everything up to get that opened. Ordered shirts for the gym, started telling people all about it. Getting social media ramped up for marketing. Things were looking up, they seemed to be getting better. We were an unstoppable team Bri and I. Man, all this shit and we were doing great, again in my eyes. During all of this I never really stopped to check on Bri and make sure she was doing alright, to find out what she wanted. Or what she needed from me.

One day I got to work, got called into the office. Walking towards it I knew what was happening. New management, I didn't get along with the managers and the way they did things and how they treated employees. I was about to get laid off. It only took them 10 minutes to do it and I was back at my desk cleaning it out. I got to my car and had to call Bri and let her know what just happened. She seemed to take it well, so I just went on about the day. I never really checked to make sure that she was good. I took it at face value, she said she was good, so she was good. Fuck I was so focused on me I am not sure that I would have paid attention to her feelings if she had told me that she was freaking out.

I started getting phone calls back to back from this number in Texas, I ignored them. You know you get a call and its not a number or from an area you know so you ignore it, sales calls, right? One day I got a voicemail from it. I listened to it and it was a woman telling me she was related to me and needed a callback. I hit my dad up and asked if he knew the number or the ladies' name. While I was waiting for a reply, I noticed I had a Facebook message from her as well as an email on my business account from her. I called her back, there was no way this was some sort of a scam in my mind.

God damn if this call didn't just hit me with more amazing news. This lady ended up being my great aunt. My dad's stepmom's sister. She had been looking for me for about a year or two. It appears that my grandfather on my dads' side had passed away. Wait for it, he had passed about three years prior. Because of the situation between my grandparents and my parents, my dad's stepmom didn't want anyone telling us that he had passed. But it appears that my grandma had fallen sick and passed away as well. When she fell sick, she had asked my great aunt to locate me tell me about my grandpa and her. She said that because I used to send them letters every year telling them about family updates, she wanted me to know and tell the rest of the family.

During that call, I also found out that my grandma had passed. Not to mention just a few months prior my dad's mom passed away. Yup, that's right in 2018 I lost my dads' mom, dad, and stepmom. All while dealing with my mom being sick, lost my job, living in another person's house, trying to start a business, and not I get to tell my dad about his dad and stepmom passing away. "Why the fuck am I going through this shit?" is all I could think.

Towards the end of June 2018, my dad started working on getting all of us out to Texas to visit them because mom was not doing well. He said that he felt it might be good for her to see all of us. We booked our flights and were getting ready and excited to see them. We planed the trip around when I had my baby girl so she could go.

July 1, 2018, I got a call from my dad confirming that we booked the tickets. He told me how mom was not doing that well, and he was afraid she might not have much more time. They had signed her up for in-home hospice care that Friday. That night I couldn't sleep, I was tossing and turning, and this time not because my son was gaming. Something in my gut was telling me that mom was hurting. At about 1 in the morning, I remember praying in bed.

"God, I know my mom is in pain, Father please take this pain away from her right now. God, if you would please just heal her right now. Rid her of her cancer. But Father if it's your will to take her home, please do that. Just rid my mom of her pain. God, take her home tonight. Amen."

I went right to bed after that prayer. I woke up again at about 3 AM, wide awake.

"God is she with you? Please tell me she is with you. Is she with you, cancer-free now?"

I got a call from my dad, panicked, crying, all he got out was *"Ed, she is gone."*. Mom passed away. He said he needed all of us to come out to Texas ASAP. I was broken. I was crushed. But Bri was right there with me to pick me up. She held me so tight with so much love, so much compassion, and comfort. God this woman was so amazing too and for me. She was always there for me and with me through all this shit and hell.

We changed our tickets; we told the kids. She told her mom, and that amazing woman that I had been such a prick to for eight fucking years came flying over to the house to help and comfort me.

July 5, 2018, we were on a plane to Texas to help dad. While out there we did what we could to help my dad get everything cleaned up and packed up and situated for him. The typical family drama happened during that time. When my brother got there Bri and I got the feeling like we were no longer needed by my dad. We just started feeling like because he was there my dad no longer needed us. Honestly a feeling I had lived with for years regarding my dad. I felt like I was a kid again, and not in a good way. I felt neglected, I felt unwanted and unneeded. Like why the fuck was I there? Comments made about me and my kids, just unnecessary stuff, especially given the reason why we were all there. Comments like "when your brother showed up, I knew at that point everything would be taken care of and things would be ok." and "Now I can finally wat a good home cooked meal." As if my wife couldn't cook?

Then the comparing of how much smarter my brother's kids are compared to mine. Never liked that when I was a kid, I still don't like that type of talk. Well we helped as much as we could, well more like we were the cleaning crew and now the "important" stuff needed to be done and we were no longer needed. Well, we came back to Georgia about a week later and started working towards opening the gym and getting our lives back on track. I got to deal with the kid's feelings being hurt by the comments that were made and the way they were treated.

When my dad came to Georgia and saw the living situation, we were in he offered to rent a house for us for a year. Bri found a house, and that whole situation was not drama-free. Too many people involved in the selection of the house Bri and I were going to live in. It seemed that some involved felt as though my baby girl didn't need a room of her own because she only saw me every other weekend. When it was all said and done, we got a house that each kid had their own room and a room for when my dad visited. Got moved in, and I thought thank God now we can rebuild. We have our own place, and everything is going to be great. The gym finally opened. I had a few clients signed up in the first couple of days. This was going to be my come back story. From nothing to something. All the Glory to God. I got an inheritance from my grandfather passing away, so we lived off that. Please note something here. I just said "I", not "we", that was my view.

Trust me I wish I could tell you all this was the end and that God took care of me right here and now. I wish I could give you a great "And they lived happily ever after." But no, I can't. That's right I wasn't done fucking shit up. Are you guys ready to hear more?

Chapter 13

Final Nail in the Coffin for Her

This one might jump around a bit, just stick with me here, please. We opened the gym in February of 2019. The gym consumed me, working six days a week, if a client was in there right before I closed, I would stay back even if it was just to talk to them about their goals. All I thought about, all I talked about was the business. It had to be daunting being around me. There were plenty of times I could have closed shop and gone home to help with whatever, but I was selfish and didn't. I was neglecting my wife and didn't even see it or notice it.

I would come home from working my dream job, and act like I was drained and had a rough day. I would always come home and say hi to her first, give her a hug and a kiss. I would ask if she needed help with anything, but did I really want to help her? I mean if she said she needed help with something I would have, but did I want to help with anything or just sit on my ass like a lazy bum? She would slave over cooking dinner, cleaning the house, taking care of our little dude. Every day she would come to the gym and spend time with me, her and little dude.

I had friends that came to the gym to work, most of my clients were friends not a lot of clients that I didn't know. I was helping people achieve what they wanted, helping them get healthy. Because they were friends if they wanted my time, I would give it to them. No boundaries ever set, not even as a businessman. People wanted a discount; I gave it to them. People wanted to come in right before closing, I would let them and then like I said, I would hang out with them. When I would get home, she would be upset, and rightfully so. I was replacing her with my business and clients.

She started coming to the gym and working out in the mornings. Mornings I normally had a few clients come in and work out around the same time, so even when she was working out, I wouldn't give her my full attention. Hell, I would even get upset that at times she would want me to watch little due while she worked out. All she needed was a break to do something for her, and I was thinking it wasn't fair. Never once did I think about how she needed time for her. Just how this was not fair what if I had a client walk in, what would I do?

A friend of mine tried telling me some insightful things about my relationship with Bri, but it was always cryptic and covered in sarcasm or jokes. So, my thick head never got it. Looking back, I can see that when Bri would come to the gym she looked down and out, just drained. But she would light up when people would come in. Every time she would pull up to the gym I would run out, client or not, to say hi and get little dude, to hug my wife and kiss her. Maybe to look good in front of people in the gym, to make her think I was amazing and caring and loving. When she looked drained or irritated, I would honestly brush it off and tell her to chill, that I was there, and I had it.

Never really had it. Again, looking back now I see all the times that Bri told me that she felt like I would side with everyone else over her. Plenty of times in the past, to "fix" an issue, there would be a problem and I would try to make everyone in the situation happy. Kids would be rude, I would justify and make excuses for the kids to Bri, and yell at the kids. This went on since the beginning of our relationship. I would brush it off, those feelings she had.

Even with my ex, I would just pacify her. It was like I could be mad and get upset, but no one else could because all that was my issue, my burden, and no one could understand, and no one could be upset but me. In a nutshell, I had zero problem-solving skills.

While I thought everything was great and moving forward perfectly, my marriage was falling apart. I was, unknowingly, emotionally detaching myself from my wife. We started getting into arguments. We would sit on opposite sides of the couch. We would have the TV on, and both be on our phones. She would be texting friends; I would be posting things about the gym. I was so stupid, I thought because we were having sex, and we both said how amazing it was, everything was great. These arguments were just little hurdles and normal. I mean hell we would high five each other after sex. How could the marriage be going down the drain if we were doing that, right?

She would ask me to sit next to her on the couch, and I would reply with "why don't you come here? Why do I always have to come to you?" After arguments, that I would keep going on for hours, to the point where neither of us could remember why we were arguing, to begin with, I could not sleep. Then I started sleeping on the couch here and there, or in the guest room.

During the arguments I would say stupid shit like *"Bri I am drained, I have nothing more to give. What do you all want from me? Do you want me to cut my wrists and drain out all my blood? Is that what you all want?"*. This was not the first time I had said things like this to her. I would point out that if she had a job, we would not be tight on money and things would be better. Then when she would ask or say she would get a job; I would tell her no that I had it. I told her if she wanted to get a job, then that's cool, but I could take care of us, I could make it all work. What mind games was I playing? I mean really what the hell is wrong with me?

One night we got into argument so bad, that I went to the living room. When I got tired, I went to the guest room. I was so full of rage at this point over stupid crap and the fact that when I tried to talk, I couldn't get any answers. Well, I could not get the answers I wanted, looking back now that was the real reason. I was in a bad place and did not want to admit it, nor did I want to admit I needed help. The help that honestly Bri could not give me.

I didn't realize it then, but I needed to be in counseling, real therapy, to help me with a lot of deep-rooted issues. Bri had mentioned it a few times, but I rejected it. Why? Well, the last few times I had been in counseling destruction followed. I had told myself many times in the past that I would never go through that again, that I could fix this all on my own. Clearly, I could not.

I remember telling her one night that I was dealing with some depression, and I could not get out of the funk for some reason. She tried to help me, but I rejected her help for some reason. I didn't even realize I had rejected her at the time. I was in self-destruction mode and I didn't know it, nor could I stop it.

One day we were talking about things, a bit heated of course because that is what I did. My emotions were out of control, I wanted to control something, anything. Bri told me that it hurt her that I did not want to sleep in the same bed as her. It made her feel horrible that her husband would rather sleep alone than next to his wife. I told her that I hated it too, but I was at a point that I did not want to be in the same bed as her, and I did not even want to have sex with her. What the fuck was I thinking? I was seeking attention. I was having a pity party. All because my actions were pushing my wife away, not that I realized it then. Why was I saying these things to the most perfect woman God had ever put in my life? Because I was not getting what I wanted. Because she had a mind of her own, and I wanted to just have things my way. Because I am never satisfied with what I have and always wanted more. When I got more, I wanted even more. Because I was a large man child. Because I was a dick of a husband. Because I hated myself for some reason.

June 2018, the worst time of my life. Bri and I were fighting just about every night, even though she was writing amazing things about me on social media when really, I was a monster bent on destroying everything in my life for some reason. One day I went home early to talk with her. I got home and we talked about the fights and what we needed to do to get back on track with a healthy marriage. Within this discussion, there were some heated moments, and I fucked up. I called her dad spineless, I told her that I did not want a divorce, but I needed to hear her say that she didn't want it either. I was pushing her into a corner.

I gotta tell you all, this is hard to write about, because it is so fresh in my life right now. I really fucked things up again. I had the most amazing, supportive, intelligent, kind, loving, spiritually connected wife a man could ever wish and pray and hope for. Yet here I am treating her like shit. I was building up the gym, adding Jiu-Jitsu classes for kids, had found a guy who I was talking to so I could add adult classes to the mix as well. Even with me treating Bri like shit, she was still so excited and supportive of the gym and the choices I was making with it.

I had a new coach in Jiu-Jitsu, we added the adult classes. He was helping me advance and get better at Jiu-Jitsu. One day he was working with me at the gym, he had a few higher ranks come in with him to help. Bri and Sydney came up to the gym with bottled water and toilet paper. I saw Sydney come in and I waved, I didn't even pay attention to see if Bri came in. Apparently, she had followed Sydney into the gym, but I was so focused on me I didn't see her for a few minutes. I looked up and saw her standing in the doorway. I smiled and waved, normally I would have gotten up and gone to my wife hugged her, kissed her, and said hello. I was so focused on me at that time I didn't do that, I just sat on the mat. I had no clue how much that hurt her feelings and how that made her feel.

June 29, 2018.

A date I will never forget. I was at the gym, did a group workout for a few people. The guy that thought he was helping me out, I mentioned him earlier, anyway, started talking to me as he was leaving the gym after the workout. He said a bunch to me, but the one thing he said to me that I cannot get out of my head was this.

He said. *"I am not good at this kind of stuff, and I am not trying to overstep any boundaries here man. You need to go home and talk with Bri. This gym don't mean shit compared to her. I think you would be willing to allow your marriage to fail before you let this gym fail."*

I told him that wasn't true, and that I was going to be able to fix my marriage. I went home and tried talking to Bri. This is when she let me know how I made her feel the evening she came to the gym and I did not get up to say hi to her. I told her I would close the gym down if she wanted. She rejected that idea, she said she would not allow me to do that. She said if she said yes to that then I would resent her for it the rest of my life. I tried assuring her I would not, but again I was not good a communicating anything.

We had plans to hang with some friends that night, I had not eaten anything since that morning. The conversation with Bri did not go the way I thought it should, so I got butt hurt and pissed. The entire drive to our friend's I hardly spoke to Bri. I got to our friends and we put on a good show like everything was ok. I had a few beers, and shots. Thought I was fine, we left their house a few hours later because we needed to get Little Dude to bed.

I don't even remember what started it, but we got into it in the car. I got pissed and told her to pull the car over. When she did, I opened the door and slammed it shut and started walking home. She was screaming at me not do leave, to get back in the car. I ignored her screams and cries for me to come back. I did this right in front of our little due.

The guy that told me *"the gym don't mean shit…"* I guess was right behind us and say this happen. He pulled up and told me to get into the car. I got in, and we talked. I was freaking out; my marriage was almost over. All he could really tell me was he tried to warn me. He asked me what I would do if I got him and Bri was gone. I told him I didn't know, and that I don't think I could live without her. Well, fuck me if it didn't get back to Bri that I was threatening to kill myself. Something that she had feared I would do because of my past.

He took me home; I was a mess, to say the least. I saw Bri when I got home, and I broke down. I was sobbing, asking her to forgive me, telling her that I was so sorry, begging her to forgive me. The look on her face will always be embedded in my head. A look of pain, hurt, disgust. She looked at me and said that she needed me to go to sleep, in the guest room. I did as she asked, but all I wanted to do was go to bed with her, fall asleep holding her hand. I just wanted her to tell me it was going to be ok and we were going to get me help and get us help. I remember praying that night.

"Heavenly Father I come to you broken and just messed up. I messed up God. I need your help. I am messing things up left and right in my life. I am selfish God, please Lord help me. Help Bri to forgive me. I need help. I need to change, I need help."

I just repeated myself over, and over again. Like a broken record. I was riddled with fear. Fear that I had just fucked things up so damn bad. I remember not falling asleep until I heard her come back inside. She had gone outside to talk to him. That scared the shit out of. My head started racing, thoughts filling my head. Insecurities rushing through my mind.

June 30, 2018.

I woke up, and she was asleep still. I went into our room and saw her sleeping. Peacefully sleeping. Like everything in her life was perfect. Honestly, I could have watched her sleep for the rest of my life. I went back to the guest room.

When she woke up, I went downstairs like I hurt puppy, walking on eggshells, tail tucked between my legs. We didn't speak that much. I noticed she was telling little dude to say things to me but not talking to me. I tried a couple of times to talk with her and it was a short one-word answer. I asked if we could go grab lunch or dinner together like we used to. Just the two of us to talk about what has been going on and fix it? She said yes but would not make eye contact with me. Throughout the day she just drifted further and further away from me. On her phone texting like crazy.

That afternoon I asked if she wanted me to ask her parents about watching little dude so we could go to dinner. She told me not to, that she was going to be going to a friend's house because she needed space. It was the house of the guy and his wife. I was crushed.

She started packing her bags. She told me she needed a couple of days to think. Little dude woke up and at about 5:30 we were in the garage, both of us crying and telling each other we loved each other, hugging and kissing. I watched my wife and son drive away. I went to my room and dropped to my knees and started praying.

"God help me, I have totally fucked up Lord. I need you to help, fix me, please. Don't let her leave me. I can change, I can be a better husband, a better dad, a better man. Please, Lord, don't let this happen again. Bring her back Lord."

That night my oldest and I talked, and he said he did not blame her. He pointed out how much of an ass hole I was. Not what I wanted to hear, but what I needed to hear.

The next week is where I completely fucked my life up. My head was racing I was not sleeping or eating. Trying to run a gym and figure out what the hell I needed to do to fix this mess I created.

I accused her of cheating on me, and the guy of it. I was whining to people about my life, I was getting questioned left and right. I felt like I owed people answers so I gave them. Just causing more destruction, completely obliterating my reputation and hers. Clients were getting sick of coming to the gym and seeing me the way I was. Some people that were close to us started giving me advice, and I was taking it. All of it, the good and the bad. I was messing up even more.

Bri moved back into the house, and I moved out on July 2nd. I went to the house to drop Little Dude off. This entire week she made sure that I had time with our little dude. I noticed she was not wearing her wedding ring. I asked her about it. She started crying and told me she wanted a divorce. She said that she loved me but was not "in love with me". I made more mistakes, not giving her space, snooping around. "Broke" into the house, I had a key, to find anything I could to see what caused this, what was going on. Went to get her phone and she woke up. I scared the shit out of her. My oldest woke and told me to get out of the house that I was fucking things up more. She called the cops on me. A huge part of me died right there. That was not the first time I had heard that. Those were the exact same words my ex said to me several years prior. Oh, and about 34 girls in high school too. I left the house, pissed off, hurt, and empty. What the actual fuck just happened, what had I just done?

According to my son, she had her dad come to help her move out that morning. That night I moved back into the house. No sleep, hardly eating. I went from 178 pounds to about 143 pounds in about 3 weeks. I started alienating people from my life. Getting pissed because I was not getting help. Turning into a selfish asshole, to say the least. Every night I prayed.

"Heavenly Father, I pray to you tonight. Please forgive me for hurting Bri. Lord, I have messed up beyond belief. I am broken Lord, please heal me. God, what is wrong with me? Why am I this way? Why can't I do things right? Why am I such a POS?"

Pity party, after pity party. Selfish beyond recognition. I was in self destruct mode for sure. Every song, commercial, movie, TV show brought me to my knees in tears. I was dealing with the one-year anniversary of my mom's death. I could not focus on anything but her. I started looking up was to change my mindset, sleep mediation videos, psychological help as well on YouTube.

I remember a could that was our friend talked to her one day. She let it all out. She told that I was mentally, verbally, and emotionally abusive to her for the entire relationship. They said that they never saw that in me. She told them that I was good at hiding it when around people. They told her that all they see right now is a man who desperately wants his bride back. With every ounce of his being, I wanted her back. Her words to them stung when I heard them.

"Well, he didn't want the marriage a month ago."

The most inaccurate statement I could have ever heard. I wanted that marriage to work every day, every second of my life. With every ounce of my soul, I wanted that marriage to work. I wanted to spend the rest of my life with her. I wanted to give my all to her, and put my everything into us. I just did not know what to do, I did not know how to properly communicate with her. I did not want to admit that I did not know that I did not have the answers, that I was doing things wrong. I figured if I could just procrastinate long enough these issues would go away. Just keep sweeping them under the rug and all would be ok. Why do we men do this? Why do we wait till the last minute to admit there is an issue? Why do we not seek help for our marriages sooner? Why can't we get our egos in check?

I was always in my own head. Telling myself, regardless of what I had in my life, that I did not deserve it, or I wanted more because what I had was not good enough, we needed better, we needed more. Never happy with what we had. Setting unrealistic expectations. That had to be taxing for her. Living with someone who was never happy with what he had.

I was happy with her, but due to my issues, I am sure she never saw it or felt it. I never did communicate it properly or timely to her.

Chapter 14

<u>Failed Attempt</u>

This is a letter I wrote to Bri one day. I wanted to put as much out there as I possibly could.

"Bri,

I am writing this letter to you in the hopes that you will see my heart. I want to start by letting you know that I know I have messed up big time with you and us. I hurt you very deeply and damaged your trust in me, as well as your love for me. I allowed my emotions and lack of understanding to get the best of me. I allowed my emotions to consume me and allowed them to control my actions. I have said that I know are not true. I did not intend for any of this to happen, meaning it was not my goal to do damage. But I know I fucked up, and I apologize profusely for this, for my words, and my actions. All I have ever wanted to do was have good communication with you and grow as a man and husband with you as my wife. I understand that I have failed in several areas of doing this with and for you. I want to apologize for disappointing you, for leaving you feeling neglected and insignificant. For making you feel like you were just a "cook" or a "maid". You are not those things; you are so much more than that. I held you to an expectation that you never agreed to, I had no understanding of how you needed and wanted to be treated. I just jumped in and started doing.

I have allowed outside influences to consume my time and distract me from you. I missed queues from you several times over the years, but I thought we had worked through some of those things, and I felt that I was doing better. I see that I was wrong. I know that all of my actions, lack of actions, and words have been devastating for you. I can't even imagine what you are thinking or feeling right now, but it has to be devastating. And writing that devastates me, to know that I did that to you. I allowed my past hurts and anger to come into our marriage, thus hurting you so I cannot blame you for your loss of trust in me. Words cannot express my remorse for what you have gone through.

Bri I know I got complacent in life. I got self-centered and focused too much on me, in an unhealthy way. This has caused me to make huge mistakes, caused me to become angry and lash out. Assumptions were made on my part, communication wasn't good between us. I couldn't find a way to express my concerns to you or the balls to even ask what was up properly.

Bri I love and adore you with all my being. You helped give me so much strength, hope, joy, and you helped rescue me in so many ways over the past 7.5 years, yet I never told you these things. You and I met that night at Lifetime fitness, and I knew then that there was something amazing about you. It had nothing to do with the outside, there was just something about you that called to me. I cannot explain it right now. I fell in love with you hard and fast. You brought so much love and joy into my heart from every text, call, and moment I spent with you.

The nights at Chick-fil-a and Starbucks were always amazing for me. I got the chance to just see your smile, see your beautiful brown eyes light up with those spots of golden yellow. Not to mention the love you showed Luke and Sydney from the first time you interacted with them. Every day my feelings for you grew, and they still do. Even through all of this, my love for you grows. I love you more than anything or anyone I have ever loved in my life. My love for you is so different than any other love I have felt in my life. I can't even come up with the words to truly explain this to you, not in writing or in conversation.

I know that you are a strong woman, you are driven, smart, and capable of phenomenally great things, and beautiful inside and out. These are just a few things that cause me to love you more and more each and every day. I know I never told you these things in a way that you could receive. You stood by my side through the ending of my divorce. You picked up the pieces of a broken family and helped build a beautiful family for Luke, Sydney, and me. You helped me fight for Luke and Sydney even when you were tired you were able to muster up the strength to help me keep pushing forward. Then we had Landon, our little blessing. You have no idea how much this little guy reminds me of you. Why? Because I have never said it to you. His love for just waking up in the morning (Mr. Sun is awake), his smile (I see so much of yours in his), the way his eyes light up (like yours do), his joy in everything he does. Even his sassy attitude.

I want more than anything the chance to work on this with you. I <u>HAVE</u> wanted to be your husband since about three weeks into our relationship, and that want has never died. Again, I know this letter seems contradictory to the way I have acted and treated you, but this is the truth from the bottom of my heart.

Again, I am simply wanting you to understand my remorse, as well as my actual love for you as a woman, human being, and my wife/friend. I have realized that it does not matter how much love I store for you in my heart, what matters more is how much love I can give to your heart. I promise never to hurt you like the way I have. I did fail you, I did not meet your expectations, and I have hurt you deeply. Again, I love you so much and I apologize."

That is exactly how I typed it out. Bad grammar and punctuation too. I remember her telling me that she got my letter and had nothing to say to me, but if I needed or wanted to talk, she would listen. I never took her up on the offer, yes again I fucked up there. I wanted so badly to see her and talk to her, but I didn't have the balls. Now I don't blame her for not wanting to talk to me, I was hateful and just not in a healthy place.

I was looking for that romance movie moment, that one that does not exist. Looking for that one thing that would make her say *"Ok let's work this out, one more chance Eddie!"*. All I wanted her to see was that I was sorry, and I wanted to work on us. But I had done so much damage, she could not see.

Chapter 15

Issues

I had issues. Well, I still have them, but I am at least working on them. One day in my Google search on how to fix me and my personal issues I ran across an ad on social media. I had already had a bunch of calls with therapists about the issues I had, what I had done to Bri. They all said they could but none of them felt right. They all went the avenue of *"We will help you get her back."*. Until one day I saw this ad for a group. A group for Christian Men going through troubles in relationships. I was done with all these *"We will help you get her back."* groups.

For some reason though I filled out the form for the free call. Got the email with some of the information. I was feeling a pull towards this group. I had my free call and it was different from the others. The lady was named Amy Hill, and she seemed cool on the phone. I told her everything I had done wrong, that I knew of. Some of what Bri had told me, and everything I could I think of. Honestly, I think my list was a lot longer than Bri's list.

By the end of the call, I was hooked. I knew this lady was going to be able to help me become a better person, father, friend, brother, uncle, person, and maybe a better husband. She told me it was a very intense program, and I liked that idea. Weekly homework, group calls, had to be open and honest or she would call me out. I could have one-on-one calls too, plus access to her via Facebook. I jumped right into the program. Watching the videos, doing the homework. Working on everything I could to start transforming myself into a new man.

S I become more involved with this group I started having guys reaching out to me asking to pray for and with them. I had a couple of guys call me in some very dark moments of their lives. I found myself talking to guys and helping them find hope, helping them find the will to continue to live. This was freaking me out, talking guys off the edge. A couple of times with a couple of guys, who were ready to end it all right then and there, ended up stepping off the ledge. They would tell me that my story spoke to them and they appreciated me sharing. They would say that I helped them find a reason to want to live.

What was going on here? I was nothing special, I hardly wanted to live, I was just existing. This wasn't me helping them, this was God using me to help them. Why me? Why this way? Every story I would hear, I would take their pain on. I had no clue what God was doing, looking back maybe He was giving me the want to live and not just exist, maybe He was showing me how much pain I felt to represent the amount of pain that I was causing people in my life just existing? *"No one likes a mopey Eddie."*

To you reading this, no one likes a mopey _____ (just put your name there). Now go work on your happy. You won't regret it, trust me.

I had so many worrying about me possibly becoming suicidal again. I can't lie, there were nights that I thought about how it would be if I was gone. What if Eddie was no longer around? Who would really care that I was gone? Yes, those thoughts started creeping in, but it was different this time. I was down in a very dark place, but somehow it was different. I hurt so much more than anything in my life, the depression was heavy. The thoughts were there, but the "want" to act was not there. Hell, the tools were there to do it as well. Knives, gun, razor blades. You name it I could have done it.

Any time the thoughts would start coming *"no one cares, they won't miss you..."* I would drop to my knees and start praying. I would think about my kids. I would think about the people that I was friends with, I could see that all I would be doing was spreading my pain to every one of them. That was not fair to them, they did not deserve any part of my pain. I would think of my daughter getting married and not having me there to walk her down the aisle. I would think of my oldest and all the Amine we watched, who would he talk to about that? My little dude, how could I do that to him, how could I let him grow up without me? No father to grow up with?

No, I would not do that, I would fight those thoughts. So again, I would pray. I would pray so much, all hours of the day, crying, angry, happy, whatever the emotion was, I would pray. After a while, the emotions and the fear, and the thoughts would go away. After a while, the thoughts become fainter. The stopped happening at all.

During this time, I tried to help a buddy out with his situation. I was in no place to help him to be honest, but that is one of my downfalls. Anyway, he had told me that he wanted to become a trainer and we agreed that he could move in with me, rent-free. He would help with the gym and use it to help get into the training industry and be closer to his son.

He came in and started making some amazing changes to the gym, cleaned it up and got some things rolling a bit. The offer was, live in my house rent-free, help at the gym. He could come and go as he needed. I tried to help him get a part-time job too. Well, I gave him some contacts to reach out to. I paid for meals as best I could. Said anything he charged a client for training we would just split 50/50. With his issues and mine combined it was a recipe for disaster.

We talked about the direction of the business over the next year. I had lost the passion to be a personal trainer. I just wanted to teach Jiu-Jitsu. I told him that he could take over the physical fitness side of the business, he came up with some amazing ideas. I started focusing on that aspect of the business, he said he would focus on the weights and boot camps and getting more clients over there on that side.

He would tell me how I was fucking things up and causing clients to feel uncomfortable. I knew I was and that is why I gave him that side of the business to work. I just had no interest in doing it anymore. Even offered him part of the business to work it.

I went out and got a job so that I could pay my personal bills as well as take care of the gym. This was not working out for him apparently; I became his personal punching bag. He would point out all my flaws, flaws I already knew about. When he would get pissed, he would lash out at me. When I would start to get pissed and stand up for myself, he would start telling me how aggressive I was and how I was not acting like a Christian. I never set proper boundaries with this guy. I looked at it this way, he was living in my house rent-free, I gave him the ability to build the fitness portion of the business to build and run. Totally upfront with how I could not pay him an hourly rate or anything and that it was all commission-based.

I was working on me, and learning what type of person I was, and what kind of persona I wanted to be. Very broken and vulnerable still. While he was working clients out, I would be at the gym working on my homework. He would point out how that was not professional.

I got a job, like I said, to pay the bills and keep things afloat. He started telling clients that I was turning the gym into a Jiu-Jitsu school, and while that was not a lie, it was not going to happen as fast as he was telling people. He was telling the members about my personal stuff, and how I was not paying him. Even though I paid him when he brought money in. I gave him half of what he brought in, just like we agreed.

One afternoon I got a call from one of the members, who was a friend, telling me he needed to cancel his membership and his wife's as well. He told me how this buddy of mine was not going to be there anymore, so it wasn't going to work not having a trainer there. I was shocked I had no clue what he was talking about. That is when he told me my buddy left. That evening when I came in after work for BJJ class, there was a note on the computer from him. He bailed on the gym. He went to the house packed his stuff and left to go back home. In the letter he pointed out my mistakes, I think I have been here before. He stated that God didn't pull him down here to be close to his son, or to get into the fitness industry. He stated that God pulled him down here to get my ass into therapy and get my life right. He stated that I needed to just turn the gym into a BJJ school and get my shit together. Oh, and he insulted my ability to raise my kids and ended it with how much he loved me and respected me.

In about 3 hours I lost every fitness member. Down to about $500 in revenue. How the hell was I going to make this thing work? I had just hired my BJJ instructor to start building an adult class. I had no clue what I was going to do. A new job, a failing business, and a divorce heading my way. I was served with divorce papers a few days before my birthday. I could not see anything positive happening in my life, it was all clouded by all the crap falling apart in my life.

At one point a friend of mine gave me an illustration of a dream she had. She said that I needed to picture my life as a house. A house that was built on a lot of sin. My childhood, my first marriage, life between the divorce and marring Bri. All that without God. She said that she saw that roof as the only part of my life being built with God. Stating at my baptism, then the wedding, then little dude. She said that I need to see God as a wrecking ball so to speak. He was breaking the house down, and He was going to rebuild a better, stronger house. It was crazy because my life coach had talked to me about how there are three types of houses we can build, and she uses the Three Little Pigs as her illustration. Straw houses and wooden houses that are weak and can be blown apart quickly and easily, and that we as men need to build strong houses on firm foundations that will be able to stand the test of time.

They were right, I had built an entire "kingdom" that was built on sin, lust, idols, selfishness, hurt, that was weak and made of straw. Easy to break into, and to be torn down. It was time to start rebuilding, with my focus on God. Allowing Him to build it with me, and to take the lead on building it.

I remember asking one day if Bri would be willing to let the divorce be put on hold? I asked if we could just see what God does. I was not asking her to pull the paperwork, just asking if we could put it on pause and pray about it and let God take over. She said that she understood what I was asking for, but she needed the divorce.

October 1st, we had our first court date for the divorce. I prayed my ass off.

"Heavenly Father I come to you right now asking you to have mercy on me. I know I don't deserve this, but can you please put the divorce on hold, please Lord don't allow this marriage to be torn apart. God, please restore our marriage. In Jesus' name, I pray. Amen"

Well, there were some issues with the paperwork, and we didn't have time to fix it. This caused a fight between Bri and me. We had another court date by the end of the day.

As if things could not get any worse, during all of this, my relationship with my daughter was crumbling. She stopped really visiting me, hardly answered my texts, started ignoring my Snapchats. Was I about to lose another person in my life? I remember one day Bri hit me up asking if Sydney had blocked her on Social media. I was not sure; I had no clue if she had. I told Bri I would "look into it". I hit Sydney up and she said that she had. She said that she could not handle seeing Bri all happy and me not being there with her. I asked if she would please just unblock Bri? I was met with the first "no" from my baby girl. She told me it was all just too much for her to handle. She wanted to see Bri and me together and seeing her without me hurt her too much.

Shortly after that, I got a call from my ex about our daughter. She said in a nutshell that I was not healthy for Sydney. She said that we needed to talk and that Sydney had things she needed to tell me. She told me that she was talking Sydney to counseling over the head of what was going on in my life and how it was impacting our daughter. This crushed me, I was hurting my baby girl. My life, my emotions, my erratic behavior was hurting her.

I met my ex and my daughter at a Starbucks. While my daughter was waiting on the drinks my ex and I sat outside. I basically got told how I was a man child and allowing my emotions to take over everything like I always did. My ex informed me that our daughter had a great session with the counselor and that she had some very hard but truthful things to tell me. I was also told how I was allowing too much of personal life to fall on our daughter. That I was the issue, and that I needed to grow up. I really didn't need to be told that, because I was already back into the stage of "everything is my fault, I am the cause of everyone's issues, etc.".

Our daughter sat down with us and basically told me that she had made the choice to not come to visit me for a while. She told me that I was hurting her by updating her about Bri and I. That all she wanted to do was be able to be a kid. She told me that she didn't care if Bri left me, and even though she would ask for updates, and ask if Bri was coming back, and if I could fix it and get her back, she really did not want to know nor did she care if Bri ever came back. She informed me that Bri was not her mom and that Bri would never be her mom. This coming from the girl who called Bri "Smomma" after the engagement. This was a nickname Sydney and her friends came up with for Bri meaning Stepmom. It took everything I had to hold back my tears. She was crushing me to hear my baby girl dismiss Bri so quickly.

On the other hand, I must say, I was very proud of our daughter for having the strength and courage to tell me these things. We ended the conversation with basically agreeing that when she was ready, she would be reaching out to me to meet up for coffee and dinner etcetera. I walked my baby girl to her mom's car. I hugged her so tight, like it was the last time I was ever going to be able to see her again, kissed her on her head and said I loved her, and I would see her later. I got in the car, I held back all my fear, anger, frustration, and tears. Prior to going and talking to her, I had told Bri that I was going to be talking to my baby girl and she asked me to call her after we talked to update her. So, I did just that. It was a strange conversation if I am being honest here. I told Bri about some of the things my ex said and Bri was quick to tell me not let anything my ex said to convince me that I am a bad person. This coming from the person who told me I was mentally, emotionally, and verbally abusive. All the same, things my ex said to me that day. That's right I was just told that I was mentally abusing my baby girl, emotionally abusing her as well.

I was so confused, was I abusive or not? Was I a man child or not? What the fuck am I, who the fuck am I? What is wrong with me? Who do I believe and who do I not believe? I just wanted to scream, punch myself in the face, rip my hair out, and yes, I just wanted to die. Not by my own hand, I was not thinking of killing myself, I just did not want to hurt anyone anymore, I did not want to exist anymore. Why live when all I do is hurt people an apparently abuse people?

I would text my baby girl just about every morning telling her I loved her, and that I hoped she had a great day. Sometimes I would get a reply, others would go unanswered. A few times she would say to me *"I love you too daddy, hope you have a better day."* Those were the best.

several times talking to Bri about Sydney and she would get upset. I would ask what was wrong and she would tell me that she hated how Sydney blocked her and she could not see her. I told her that I was working on it. She told me that she never wanted Sydney to feel like she had abandoned her, but that is exactly how Sydney felt.

November 7th, 2019 was for sure the worst day of my life. That was the day my second divorce went through. It only took a few hours sitting in the courtroom, and about 10 minutes standing in front of the judge and done. I had failed again. Failed at another marriage, failed to be a good husband, failed to keep a family together, failed to keep my wife happy and in love with me. I hear a lot of people say, *"Eddie you can't take all the blame on you."* And I get what they are saying, but I had a part in the destruction of my marriage too, and I am taking ownership of that. I did not pay attention to what my wife was trying to tell me. I need to admit that I needed help early enough. I rejected her offers to help, and suggestions to get help. Yeah, I failed her, and our children, her parents, and her family. I failed to communicate with her, I talked a lot, but I did not communicate in a loving and caring way. Listening well was not a thing I did well, I heard people talking, but listening to what they were saying? Not really my thing. I would hear what I thought the issue was, then I would try to come up with the "fix".

I had to tell my baby girl that the divorce was finalized, but I did not want it to hurt her, so I called my ex to try and figure out what we needed to do and how we should approach this with our daughter. Well, let's just say that I was down and out. I remember my ex saying something about not wanting to kick me while I was down. My brilliant response was something like *"fuck it, I am already as low as I can get, just kick me. Go for it."*

In a nutshell got told again that I was not healthy for my baby girl to be around, and that while I may not be the full cause of all of her pain, I was a major cause. She also told me how my baby girl wanted to know why I allowed their relationship to be destroyed? My ex and I decided that we would just come out and tell my baby girl the divorce was finalized.

When my baby girl got put on the pheon to talk to me, well speakerphone that is. I told her that the divorce was finalized, she took it well. I asked if she had anything to say? Honestly, I don't remember all the exact words that were said. The theme was this though.

"Daddy you are the reason for my issues, I cannot trust you anymore, you only care about Bri. You are the reason I have not had a relationship with my mom, you and Bri caused that to happen to me. Why would you do that to your daughter?"

Fuck me, why would I do that? What kind of monster does that? What sick and twisted piece of shit destroys people's life? This kind of guy, that's who. I remember her mom asking her if she wanted to continue to try and build a relationship with me and my baby girl answered with *"not really, I am fine with where it is right now. Maybe one day. Just not right now."*

She started talking to me about how she had been thinking of hurting herself, and how it was my fault because that was the kind of remodel I was. She told me that she was not sure if she could trust men because of me.

What the hell had I done? What had I done to my princess, my baby girl?

Here I was a pathetic mess of a man, just leaving a trail of pain and devastation. My wife left me; daughter wanted nothing to do with me. I could not see clearly in anything I did. Yet somehow some of the men on the counseling page I was part of saw me as an inspiration. I posted things about how fucked up I was and how bad things were in my life. Pity party? Maybe. Mainly I was trying to point out that I was just messed and trying what I could to move forward and start living so that I could try to rectify some of the mistakes I was making.

One night my baby girl asked if she could grab dinner with me and her brothers. I was elated by the request. I jumped on the opportunity to see her. We picked her up at her mom's house and had Mexican for dinner at our favorite place. She was talking about there was this guy that she liked. Let's stop right there, listen I know I am not the nest example of a man alright. But no guy is good enough for my baby girl, none. Ok, dad rant over. She was talking about a few issues she was having in the realm of life. We were in the car talking about it on the way to take her home. I remember telling her

"Baby girl, listen to me, I have failed at a lot, especially relationships."

I saw the look she was giving me in the rearview mirror.

I said, *"I am not talking about just your mom or Bri ok. Listen I had a lot of girlfriends in high school and I messed them all up too."*

She goes, *"Daddy how many girlfriends did you have in high school?"*

"Well let me think about that for a second."

I started counting and let's just say that I struggled to say the answer.

"Daddy, how many girlfriends did you have?"

"Umm, not including your mom?"

"Yes!"

"34"

"When did you start dating, like how old were you?"

"15 and a half."

"And you met mom at 17?"

"Yep!"

"34 girlfriends in 2 and a half years??"

"Yes, baby girl."

"You were a man-whore dad!"

Well, there is that. I had to explain that every single one of them dumped my ass. Because of me. What is the point of this? What point was I trying to make to her? Well, we forgot because we started making jokes about how many girlfriends and failed relationships I had. Sorry, no great life lesson there for my baby girl. Maybe for me, maybe for you. Make sure that you are paying attention to the people in your life, listen to them and their feelings. Don't just hear the words they are saying. That night I sat there thinking about all the reasons I was given by these girls as to why they broke up with me. One common reason was that I did not pay attention to them the way they wanted or needed.

Chapter 16

Brother Al - Boom!

This chapter is dedicated to my brother Al. Not my blood brother, but my brother in Christ. While this may be one of the shortest chapters I am writing, it just has a lot of meaning for me.

In the counseling group, I joined there were a lot of men going through what I was going through. Some seemed to be going through a lot more than me, and others had gone through what I was going through and they were making tremendous changes in their lives. Some were even restoring their lives, families, and marriages. The biggest thing that I noticed in this group was the number of Godfearing men working on themselves to become better men.

Lots of prayer requests, lots of fear, pain, sorrow, and love. Right from the get-go, this one guy stood out to me. He seemed like he was the leader of the pack. Not the "owner" of the page or group, just a guy who was on point. I started to look up to this guy, man he seemed to have his shit together, and he had answers, FYI I still look up to this guy. His name is Al, some of us call him Brother Al.

This guy has changed my life in so many ways. I don't think I will ever be able to thank him enough. I wish I could just point out one thing he did that changed me, but that would be diminishing everything he did and continues to do for me.

We chatted on Facebook on the group a few times, then via Facebook messenger. We exchanged numbers and that's when shit got real. Man, he would call my ass out in a heartbeat if I was having one of my pity parties. I mean I hardly knew the guy and one night he basically pointed out all the shit I had done wrong. It was amazing, very humbling. Point me in check. Where was this guy my whole life?

There were times where we would just hit each other up and not even post on the group page. We would just speak the truth to each other. There were nights that I would be down, praying, and the next thing I know my phone is ringing. It was Al. Like God was telling him to check in on me. Every time I would thank him, he would say to

"Bro this is helping me more than you know." Or *"Bro this is for me."*

Like I was doing something for him?

Now I have a bad habit of saying this like "dude" and "solid", lots of slang. His thing is "Boom". We would celebrate victories with each other. He would respond with "Boom" and I would respond with "solid". I even noticed we said it so much that the guys on the page started quoting us with our catchphrases.

NO MORE PITY PARTIES BRO!

Right before Thanksgiving, we challenged each other. A thirty-day challenge to text each other things we were grateful for throughout the day. We have been doing this every day even up to this day I am writing this chapter. This has helped me to focus more on God and his blessings that he hands me daily.

In a short amount of time, this man has helped me open my eyes to what I had done to some amazing people, and he has been helping me to not dwell on all of it. It is hard to explain how this all helped me grow. What I can say is that I thank God daily for putting this man in my life.

I started a daily devotional, *Jesus Calling* by Sarah Young. What an amazing book. You start whatever the date you get it. It has a little something for you each day of the week. I would get up and send Al a picture of that day's page. There was nothing in it for him to have reached out to me. We did not know each other, but in the short amount of time we have known each other, he knows so much about me, and I know so much about him. It's almost like we have known each other for years, not months.

So, if you don't have a Brother Al in your life, go find one. Trust me, you will thank me later for it.

Al, my brother, thank you for calling me out. Thank you for the texts and phone calls. Telling me how it was, praying for me. The challenges my man. This chapter does not do you justice. I told you that I would write this book and you would have a chapter in it my man. I can't wait to see what God does in you, through you and for you. Much luv bro. Boom!

Chapter 17

Nightmares

Not that I ever slept that well before, but when Bri left I could not sleep at all. Not for the normal reasons, but it was just a flood of nightmares. Some vivid and colorful. Some quick like flashes. But everyone tormented me so bad I wake up and just did not want to close my eyes. Because when I did, I would see them again.   Then when I had no more energy to stay awake, I would crash, and there they were again. Repeating themselves, every night.

I tried figuring out what they meant, tried praying about them, talking to people about them, nothing. Just a nightly rerun of them. Most of them had to do with my death, not my taking my life, but someone else killing me. Others had to do with me not being able to "save" Bri from harm. My emotions were so out of control that I would go three and four nights without sleep.

In my dreams I would be at the gym, no one around, always a beautiful day outside. I would be closing the gym and as I went to the front door to leave, a guy would come in. He was familiar, as in a knew him and was comfortable with him coming in. He would pull a gun out and shoot me in the gut right by my ribs on the righthand side. I would come to and he would be dumping my body in the church parking lot. I could see my blood pouring out of the bed of his truck. He would speed off kicking dirt and rocks all over me. I would take my phone out of my pocket and call Bri. Then she would be there telling me that it was ok, she was there, and she would help me. Then I was back in the gym, and it would happen again. But this time not only did I get shot the guy pulled a knife out and cut my ribs open and ripped one out. Dump my body in the church parking lot again and speed off. There she was again, holding me, telling me it was going to be alright. Then I would be back in the gym. This time after shooting me and stabbing me, ripping my rib out, dump me in the parking lot, then he would just stomp on my face. Each dream he would do this three times, then I would wake up in a puddle of sweat. I had this dream about three or four times a week. That will mess a guy up big time. One night I woke up feeling my ribs, turned the lights on to make sure I was not bleeding. Crazy right?

I mean I am sure that plenty of people have dreams like this and I am sure it was just the stress, depression, anxiety and all that causing these dreams, but I figured why not share this. Maybe someone else is allowing these types of dreams to ruin them. I could have allowed it to cause me to just stay in bed, or at the house. But I decided to just keep pushing forward.

I remember one night thinking that maybe this was the devil trying to mess with me. Trying to push me back to those suicidal thoughts. I got so pissed. I started praying for God's protection that night. Then I started telling the devil he could not win, he could not beat me, he could not have my soul. I told him that if he wanted he could come to my room that night and try to take me on. Stupid right? Calling the devil out like that? I mean what was I thinking? As many of you who are reading this book, if you made it this far, can tell, I am not the smartest person out there. I do plenty of stupid things. And this one right here has got to be on the dumbest things I had ever done. I told the devil to show himself to me so I could kick his ass. I told him that I was a fighter, and I was ready to fight him and all his little candy ass demons. I literally told him to "Bring it! Come after me and leave my family alone."

Well, let's just see what happened that night. It was July 31st, 2019. I will never forget that night and this nightmare. It shook me, no it royally fucked me up for about 3 weeks, just about every night I would have this one. In the dream, I was told that Bri wanted a divorce. We fought about the divorce in my dream for a few days. Her parents were not helpful in this dream as if they wanted me gone.

I had to go to some strange house to get things. Bri would not talk to me. This house had lots of doors to one room, like a great room so to speak. A friend of ours was there, and we went to the room to talk to Bri. She was curled up on the floor not acting like herself, like not happy, not pissed at me. She was wrapped up in a red knit blanket. It was her, but not her. Mumbling, and acting childish and terrified of something, but it was not directed at me. Talking kind of crazy. I would ask her a question and it was like she was unable to answer, like when you ask a 2-year-old a question.

I asked her in the dream if we could work on fixing us and our marriage. She couldn't or wouldn't answer the question. When I made eye contact with her in the dream, it was not my wife's eyes. The golden-brown was not there. She looked crazy or insane and void of life. She got up and walked to another room mumbling still wrapped in the blanket. The mumbling turned into a silly, giggling mumble.

I went to find our friend because she was no longer in the room with Bri and I. I could not find our friend. I went back into the room to get Bri, and she was gone. I could not find her in any room.

I saw the red knit blanket move in another doorway, so I ran to that room. When I got there, she was nowhere to be found.

There was a sickly-looking young lady in a bed with monitors hooked up to her laying in a bed in the middle of the room. She looked at me and said. "She is in there." And pointed to a door.

The panic and fear I was feeling in this dream at this point were so real, I could feel it take over my body.

I opened the door and she was not there. It was a closet and it was full of these red knit blankets. I turned and yelled at the young girl asking her where Bri went.

An older black lady was now in the room. When I looked at her, I was filled with even more fear. She walked, more like floated towards me, very quickly.

I remember feeling in that dream that this older lady knew where Bri was. There was something that just felt evil about this lady. I didn't like the feeling of her.

She kind of slithered over to another door. The blanket was sticking out of the door. I felt Bri and her presence. The old lady opened the door and I saw Bri. She looked horrified and called to me asking me to help her. There was so much fear in her eyes, there were piercing my heart and soul.

The old lady quickly entered the closet with Bri. I ran towards the door and reached for Bri to get her. I felt pure evil in that dream, it was so real. The door shut quickly and when I opened it Bri and the old lady were gone. Just the blanket was on the floor. I slammed the door shut.

That's when I woke up in a panic. My heart was racing like I had just rolled for a solid hour or ran a marathon. I jumped out of bed and latterly walked around the house looking for Bri. I could feel all the fear from that dream. I was breathing so hard I was almost hyperventilating. I was drenched in sweat, the sheets were soaking wet too. It was so real and was just a representation of how bad I had messed up. The evil I felt in that dream was embedded in my head for weeks. I could not close my eyes that night.

It is hard to explain what I felt in that dream, or when I woke up, but it was like it was not a dream but real life. Like I had experienced it in real life. For days I thought I was crazy, or at least going crazy because of how real that dream was.

For about a week I would lay in bed at night, unable to sleep, with the lights on and music playing, yes worship music, and my gun loaded on the nightstand in case that lady showed up. I was convinced she was real and coming for me. I was paranoid for sure. Because if something evil came into my room, unloading a 9mm was going to be the right thing to do.

Chapter 18

What's Next?

I was feeling really messed up physically, emotionally, mentally at this point in my life. I had to start getting back on track. I got back into my counseling homework. Starting diving deeper into my faith. I could hardly eat; it was like a chore to eat. My jaw would hurt just chewing. I was training Jiu-Jitsu again under my new coach Robert Peters. What an amazing soul this guy is. I was teaching kids how to defend themselves when needed. I had to get back on track. What was next for me?

I started making small goals to try and achieve. Get my fourth stripe on my belt. Check got that. Next train hard to get that purple belt. Ok, grow the business, focus on the job as well. I had to get healthy again for my kids. I would do what I could to try and find ten good things about every day. I was told to find 10 good things about me, but since I was failing at that one, I changed the task.

Being part of that group has been a wild trip. Talking to guys going through what I was going through was heart-wrenching. Reading prayer requests of these men, seeing how broken they were, the pain they were going through, then add my pain to the mix. It was overwhelming at times. There were nights that I would be doing great, having a great day and I would go to the page to see how guys were doing, and their pain became mine.

I am not saying that I am an empath or anything, at least I don't think that I am, but then again, I guess you could say I am still learning who and what I am. I know a lot of people have told me and will say *"Eddie you are a child of God."* And I get that. But there is more to that, I think. I mean I am a dad, I am a coach, I am an abusive husband, I am a bad example to my kids, I am a horrible ex-husband. Still working on that as you can see. I will get back to that.

What was next for me, what was I going to do, what is going to happen to me, what more devastation and destruction is coming my way? Was a capable of making the needed changes to start reconciling anything I destroyed? Listen I know it is not all my fault, but what I did had a major part to do in everything that I have been through. Taking ownership of my actions, thoughts, and what not is very important. This is how I was going to start building my road map to correct things and get my life back on track.

Over the next few months, there were plenty of ups and downs, that's life right? One of the major changes I have made is to focus on God more. Praying when the emotions would get out of control, working on giving it all to him, and listening to what he was telling me. Most of the time it was like talking to a wall in a room of a million people screaming at me. I felt like I had been sending God a bunch of texts and he was just leaving me unread.

I just wanted to know what He had in store for me. I wanted to know where to step next, which direction to go, how fast or slow. I wanted Him to send His angels down like Old Testament style, lights and trumpets blaring. Man, could you imagine that? Waking up in your deepest of sleep and behold, an Angel of the Lord in your room? Speaking to me, telling me what I needed to do next. I think about that, would I do it? Would I ignore it? Something to think about, I guess.

Again, I started making small goals for myself with my job, my business, my family, and my mental and emotional health. I started to get back on track with the homework from my counseling. Really hunkered down to find wins every day in all the shit that was going on. I started learning how to treat people better, learning how to set boundaries with people in a healthy way. Rebuilding a relationship with my baby girl.

So, we can fast forward through some more shit that happened during this time. We got evicted from the rental house we were living in. Money was very tight, and I just could not seem to get things in order, my head was still so clouded. I also learned how much I procrastinate; I also had a hard time asking people for help.

My son slept in my gym, my dad was living with us at the time and so he slept in his RV, I was sleeping at a friend's place. Now my oldest had the option to sleep at another friend's place, but he needed to do his thing. He needed his space and he needed to process. All our stuff was in a storage unit, in the cars, in the gym. We got an apartment, got our stuff moved into the apartment all within a week. My days went like this, work, teach class, move stuff into the apartment, fall asleep, have nightmares, wake up and listen to music till I had to go to work, rinse and repeat.

Christmas was coming up, and my dad was heading to Virginia to visit my brother. He needed to get away I know, and I understand completely. I was a mess and need in a good place. I was bringing everyone down with me.

My baby girl went to Australia for Christmas, but before she left, we went out on a date. Date nights with her are the best. We talked about what was going on in our lives and how I felt like I was doing better, she said she noticed a good change in me and that she liked it. We talked about what she said to me on November 7th and how she felt and how I felt. It was awesome to hear her feelings and what she needed from me. We went to Starbucks to get her a drink before I took her home. Things were going awesome with her. Then I felt it, something was off, something not good was building up in me. It was starting to hurt in my chest, I was starting to become short of breath. Lots of pain in my chest, shortness of breath, my heart was pounding, I started shacking.

I remember thinking to myself that I had this under control, I could get her home, then park the care till this went away. Started going numb, then chills, then hot flashes. Like the perfect storm was hitting me for some reason. She noticed and asked if I was ok. I told her I was fine, and I was going to get her home, her house was just around the corner.

My daughter is amazing, at this moment she said to me, *"Daddy how about you pull the car over. Let's just talk."* So, I did. She looked at me and said to breathe with her. Tears were running down my face, honestly, I was freaking out, I could not control or stop the trembling. Was I having a stroke or a heart attack? Was this a panic attack? I didn't want my baby girl seeing me weak like this. She needed a strong role model and that needed to be me. I remember her telling me to breathe and then she said to count with her. She was so calm, and I was not. We started counting, and she kept saying to me to count with her. I started to feel better, I could take a full breath with less and less pain in my chest. I stopped shaking, kind of felt normal. I looked and all I could see was my baby girls' smile.

She said, *"That wasn't that bad now, was it? You feel better?"*

I thanked and told her how much I loved her. We talked a bit more in the car in that parking lot. She told me that all she wants to see is me happy. She said that whatever would make me happy to just go for it. Her words to me still ring in my head.

"Daddy I am here for you; you will always have me. You are strong and you can do anything. If you really want something, then do the work. Make the changes you need to make and go for it. Sorry for saying this but man up and fucking go for it. Don't let anything or anyone stop you. I will always have your back. You have always put others before you, but that has taken from you. It has made you have to focus on everyone and everything all at one time. You could not keep anything going. Focus on you and what you want for once. You can do this; you can do anything. I love you. I know you miss her; I know you love her, and I know you love me. I miss her too; we all miss her. But daddy you have to start loving yourself more."

This was a pivotal moment for me. I knew exactly what she was talking about. I knew right then and there what I wanted, what I needed to do, and that I could start doing it.

Thank you, baby girl.

Christmas day 2019, my second Christmas without my family together. No baby girl, no Bri, no little dude. What was I going to do, how I was going to deal with it? Well, I spent the day watching Netflix. I found myself a good show to watch and I binged that bad boy. Just chilled out and relaxed. My BJJ coach and his family invited Luke and me over for dinner, so we went over and had an amazing time just hanging out and talking, watching BJJ competitions on TV. Life lessons go train Jiu-Jitsu, it helps.

It is an amazing community, and your teammates care, they become family.

Somewhere around this time, my oldest and I had a talk about me and my jokes. I have a dark sense of humor, lots of death jokes. One day I was making a joke and he looked at me and goes

"Not funny dad, Not funny at all. I know you are trying to be, but it's just not working."

"Dude it's just a joke, you know that, right?"

"No, dad. I don't. Sydney doesn't either."

"Ouch!"

"You don't know how often we see you and think, is this going to be the time dad snaps? Are we going to come home and find him dead? Do you understand this?"

I promised I would stop; I honestly had no clue that I was doing that to them.

Chapter 19

Prayer Time

Since the day Bri left me I have prayed every night, and just about every morning. Here are several of the prayers that I have prayed. Feel free to make them your own if you would like. They have helped me, and others have said that they have helped them. Some of these prayers I wrote for my brothers in my counseling group. Now I am not saying that I am the most powerful prayer warrior out there, or that my prayers have all been answered. No, I am not saying that at all. These are just my thoughts and prayers and words I put out there for God to hear me being open and honest with Him. They are in no real order, just prayers I wrote down on paper, or on the Facebook group.

Nightly prayer time with my little dude is one of the best times. Every night I have him we pray before bed. It is the prayer that Bri started with him. Oh, and just so you know, in case I have not already mentioned this "Wuwu" is Sydney and "Bubba" is Luke. Still to this day little and I pray this prayer, we add people to it here and there, but for the most part this is it. I will not stop praying this little guy.

> *"Dear God, Thank you for today. Thank you for protecting me and keeping me safe. Thank you for Momma, Dada, Bubba, and Wuwu. Please protect me while I sleep.*
>
> *In Jesus' name, I pray, Amen.*
>
> *Thank you, God. Thank you, Jesus."*

A very pissed off prayer.

> *"Ok God let's get real here. I am fucking up I know, but where the hell are you in all this crap? I believe you are real; I know that what your word is true. My life is falling apart, and you are just sitting there. What the hell is going on? What am I doing wrong, how do I fix this? How am I supposed to have faith in You and Trust You when my life is falling apart again? There I said it. I don't trust you, God. I am sorry but this all sucks. I want to trust You, I really do. But I just don't trust you to take care of me and my family. Help me to trust you, God. Please help me. I can't take anymore devastation in my life, no more pain. This is too much for me to take. I don't want this*

anymore. Please God, help me fucking trust
you. Or hell, just take me now, take me
home, put me out of all this misery, protect
everyone I know from this monster I am.
Take me out. I have no reason to be here
because all I do is fuck up everything, I
destroy every blessing you give. Stop this
pain now. Help me! Amen."

A prayer of thanks.

"Heavenly Father I thank you for an amazing
day filled with emotional ups and downs. The
emotional rollercoaster was amazingly scary
and joyful. Thank you, Dad, for walking with
me today. Comforting me through my
emptiness today. You moved the familiar
feelings you calmed the anxiety and pushed
it back so I could go out and be with friends.

Thank you, Jesus. Thank you, God.

Amen"

This one was for a bunch of guys in my counseling group. Well me too. I was starting to see that I had truly been making things and people idols in my life. Putting everything in front of God.

" Heavenly Father I come before you tonight
with a humble heart. We men are broken we
need you. So many of my brothers are
struggling. Questions, doubts, fears. I am not

excluded, Dad. I don't know what may come tomorrow. Something good, something bad, both? All I am sure of is this. That regardless of what comes my way tomorrow You will be there with me. And I am becoming better at excepting that this may be the case for the rest of my years on this earth.

I want nothing more than You and Your will Dad. The rest is icing on the cake for me. Yes, I want my finances back in order, yes, I want a place to call home, yes, I want my bride back, yes, I want a relationship with my kids. But Dad if none of this comes to fruition, that is fine as long as I have You.

Sure, Dad, there are times that I focus on the pain and loneliness. And it hurts. But then I talk to you and it starts to fade away.

Dad if I spend the rest of my years homeless. Living in a car or even on the streets... I am fine with that as long as I have you.

Dad, heal my brothers. Please continue your work in them. At the same time Dad, I ask that you heal them. Realtor their marriages. Bring them back together with their wives. Please don't allow them to feel the pain I feel. Don't allow them to go through what I have gone through and am still going through. Protect them. Help them see and understand. Help them start doing for their brides what we all should have been doing since the day we met them.

*Do a mighty work in them Dad. Bring
miracles to their lives tonight Dad.*

I pray this in your holy name Jesus. Amen."

Another one for my brothers.

*"Heavenly Father I pray to you tonight
thanking you for everything. Too many to
things to sit here and list them all out. Father
thank you for another day, thank you for
time with my boys today. Thank you for my
dad who has in his own way been helping me
out. Thank you for the rough times he is
causing. It is still helping me grow and show
my oldest son that I am changing. I know I
slipped a few times this weekend Dad, please
forgive me for not leading properly.*

*Dad thank you for the time with her today.
The text conversations, the fact that she
allowed me to help her today. Thank you so
much. Dad, I have no clue what you're doing
in me but thank you so very much.*

*I know in the past I have been down and out,
and I wanted to end it all. I know I tried for
two years to end it all. I haven't wanted to
live for a long-time dad. I have even begged
you to take me then. When you blessed me
with your daughter, I stopped thinking of
doing it on my own. When she left Dad, I
again just wanted you to take me home to
be with you. But today Dad I declare it I want*

to live. I may not be happy Eddie all the time. I still have my downtimes. My frustration kicks in and I start to boil over. I am so sick and tired of one step forward and twenty steps back. That is why I still push forward. I continue to push forward. I will push harder and harder every damn day to move forward. At the same time Dad, I am working on resting in Your promises.

Dad, I am terrified yet excited to let this all go to You and just sit back and watch what You do.

I pray for my brothers. Dad, speak to them all daily and guide them down the path You need them to walk. Comfort them all on their journeys when they feel down or burnt out. Help them to dig deeper than they ever have before.

Dad, I pray for your daughters. I pray that you protect them. Comfort them as well.

Dad, I pray for her tonight. Please help her with what she is going through. Please help her where she needs it. You know what she is dealing with at her parents' house. Dad, I know you can fix it or put the right man in her life to help. If that man is me, I will do what you tell me to do. If it is another then help her see it.

I pray all of this in your holy name Jesus. Amen."

While my marriage was finished, I still prayed for men going through what I had just gone through with all the hope I had inside of me, that God would help them.

"Heavenly Father I pray to you tonight thanking you for so many things. Dad oh how I have messed things up, yet you are still showing me there is hope. I receive that hope. I have hope. I trust you Dad. I trust that you are going to make things better. What things?? I have no clue, but it will get better and I know it.

Dad, I pray right now for every single marriage represented on this page. I pray blessings upon blessings over them. Dad, I claim it again and again tonight. I claim victory over the enemy tonight. He is trying to rip us apart one by one, but he messed with the wrong group of men. He picked me to mess with. He picked my bride to mess with. He may have won a few rounds, but there are many more to go. And I have more to dish out then he even knows. Dad tonight you gave me so much I can't even explain or describe or list out. So again, I say I have hope that things are going to get better and I trust you Dad.

My brothers and I come to you just asking that you continue to give us the ability to move forward in this battle and accept the things we did wrong. I ask that you help us correct the wrongs we did. No more blaming our wives for our childish actions. No more procrastination. No more whining.

I again claim victory in our marriages and the restoration of them. I will continue until the end of time. You said Yes to us once Dad. You said Yes to these marriages. How can we turn away from your blessings?

So, we fight for them now.

Thank you, Dad.

In Jesus' name, I pray. Amen."

Just being honest with our Father.

"Heavenly Father I pray tonight thanking you for keeping my emotions calm today. Dad, I have no clue what you're doing with my life. I have no clue what your plan is Dad. I am lost in this entire thing. I had ideas, wants, desires. But none of that happened today. Am I mad, sad, confused? Yes, I am. But I know something is being done. I know you have something for me. But I know I can never fully receive it until I change and grow.

Dad my brothers on this page need to grow and change as well to stop what happened with me today from happening to them. Dad soften their hearts. Open their eyes and ears. Help them hear you and your guidance.

Help the men of this world open their eyes to what we are doing to our wives and our families. Help us change and grow. Bring more men to this group earlier than I came. Help us men in this group to tell others about this program. Open our eyes to see who needs help sooner.

Dad, I love and trust you.

In Jesus' name, I pray. Amen."

I can get a little dramatic in my prayers I know. I guess this one was also me coming to terms with the fact that I was going to have to admit that I failed Bri and my covenant, and our children.

" Heavenly Father, I'm sitting here trying to figure out how to pray and what to pray for. It is coming in slowly, not really flowing like it normally does. My mind is clouded tonight, filled with confusion. The moments of joy are coming but slip away quickly because I focus on the wrong things. But what is amazing is that you are here with me. I know this because I am still here, and I am not bleeding out emotionally right now. I have been praying for what I want Dad... no clue or care what you really want for me. Just my selfish wants, and yet you still bless me with my children, with sales at the job. I focus on me and my pain a lot, which causes me to draw my focus away from you and your plan.

Yet you still bless me over and over again. Thank you, Dad... Thank you, Jesus!!

I have so much to be thankful for, yet I focus on the few things I don't have which hardens me and my heart towards you Dad, I am so sorry for my selfish actions. Dad the past 41 years are filled with sin, examples of what not to do in life, relationships, work, everything. Yes, admittedly there are times when I think I should have pulled that trigger over 9 years ago. So damn selfish of me to think that Dad, I am sorry for having even tried to do that. The pain that caused so many people who knew me then and know me now who were not even around when I was in the place. I had no clue what the heck I was doing. I had no clue, even though I didn't do it, that it would cause people pain to know I even tried. The worry and pain of a selfish thought and actions have pledged my life and relationships ever since then.

I love how I can show you all my pain, all my anger, all my torment, all my negativity, sadness, depression, and hatred... and yet you still love me Dad. Dad, I want what I want, and you give me what I need. And I have been so unthankful for that. But no more Dad, no longer am I going to sit in my own filth and darkness and self-pity.

I need your help, Dad. I can forgive anyone and everyone for anything and everything, yet I have trouble forgiving myself. I have trouble not hating myself. Help me to truly forgive myself. Why Dad? Why am I this way? Why is it so damn hard to forgive myself?

Lord the words in this song I am listening to right now speak volumes to me, and they are what I am feeling right now... "I wanna bleed I wanna feel, I wanna scream I wanna feel"... Dad, I want to bleed out all my pain and negativity, I wanna feel joy and peace... I wanna scream and let it all out... I want to feel alive again, filled with your Holy Spirit like I did 8 years ago, coming up on 9. I wanna feel whole again, not empty and void and numb.

Dad tomorrow at 9:00 AM I know you will be there with me; I know it... but I also fear that I will ignore you and your words and direction. This new chapter is freaking me the explicit word out of me.

All of this to say, Dad... Stop the pain for them, stop the bleeding Dad. Please heal them, heal their families. I got this pain because I have you, I am used to this pain at this point. But I don't like to see my brothers going through this crap, please stop their pain. I have been here before and I made it because of You, I just again ask that You stop their pain, they do not deserve this. You have made me to handle this, I have handled it for the better part of 41 years. I beg you, Dad, don't let any of them go through this any longer. I submit to you Dad, I submit my heart, my thoughts, my family, my marriage, my life, my everything I submit to you Dad.

I pray this in Jesus' Holy name. Amen."

This was after we got evicted from our rental house.

"Heavenly Father I come before you tonight humbled, but head held high. Dad, we may have done a lot wrong in the past, but you have forgiven us. Now the enemy wants to keep us focused on our past but no longer will we allow him to do that. My wife has divorced me, I have lost my house, my oldest and I are living in different places. I'm not sure I have a spot for my little dude when I get him next.

But I have You and you have me. And that is all that matters. Because the enemy can keep taking things away from me. I don't care. Because he can't take you away from me.

Dad, I pray tonight for you to help rebuild me. I need more confidence. That is all I am asking for if the confidence to keep pushing forward at my job. I have lost the grip of my confidence. I need that back so I can keep my head afloat.

Dad, I pray that you give my brothers the strength to keep pushing forward. Help us all be bright shining lights for others out there.

So they can all see who you are and what you do for your children.

Use me more Lord. Use me and my brothers and our situations to show those that don't know you who you really are.

I pray this in Jesus' holy name. Amen."

So lost right here.

"Heavenly Father I come to you tonight looking for guidance. As well as asking for You to guide my brothers. I kind of feel stuck where I am at. Like nothing I do is really moving me forward, not really moving backward either I don't think Dad? I am so ready to move forward Dad, forward with whatever your plan is for me. I am reading, I am listening, I am praying, I am seeking... but nothing that I can wrap my mind around. Is this peace, is this contentment? I don't know and I don't care because at least it is not in that hole I have been in too many times.

Dad is this where you need me now? Is this where you need us right now?

I have people in my ear telling me "forget about her...", "she doesn't care or want anything to do with you...", "she is a mess bro..". All I keep telling them is "When God tells me to stop I will."

Dad, I am sitting, I am waiting for You to guide, speak, or something. Honestly, though the silence is deafening. Talk to me Dad. Speak to us in a way that we can know it is You. Because I don't want to move unless I know the direction is coming from you. But sitting still is the hardest thing for me to do. So many things that need to get done "or else", so many directions to go, so much looking like it is all about to come crashing down again Dad... I know my brothers are seeing and feeling the same things. But for me, I don't get it Dad, for me I am just sitting here like "come crashing down!" because at least that would give me something.

Protect us and our family's tonight Dad, heal us and our families. Bless us Dad. Show us a glimpse of what you need from us so we can work towards that Dad.

In Jesus' name, I pray. Amen."

I was so sick of seeing and hearing about divorce during this one. I was trying to find reasons to forgive myself, but I could not.

"Heavenly Father I pray to you tonight thanking you for every second of my life. Thank you for today Dad. You showed up today at work. Yes, things didn't go as well as I hoped but you were there Dad. Things didn't get done today the way I had wanted outside of work, but some tasks got

completed. Thank you for that Dad. Because of that, I am not able to sleep in my own bed at the apartment but what is awesome is I still have a place to stay that is warm and has a bed and warm running water for a shower tomorrow morning. Thank for that Dad.

I know I had expectations of certain people stepping up and helping get things done. But they didn't and that is ok because others jumped in and help me in an area, I didn't know I needed help. Thank you for that Dad. Their help enabled me to get some things taken care of. It also allowed me time to talk with my oldest son. Thank you for that time with him tonight Dad.

You show up in amazing ways. And for that I am grateful. Even though I have not gotten what I wanted I have received what I needed from you Dad.

Dad, I still ask that you help my brothers on this page. Help them open their eyes to what they need to do. Help them with their marriage's tonight Father. Bless their socks off in a way that can only be explained by "wow look at what God did".

I thank you, Dad, for the ability and opportunity to pray here on this page every night for my brothers and their families and marriages. Dad, I know you will do something amazing here for the men on this page.

Dad, I pray for her tonight. I pray you give her strength. I pray that you show her your love. I pray that you bring the man into her life that she needs to be with and that will take care of our little dude the way he needs taken care of. If that is still me praise you, Lord. If that is another man and a stepfather for my little dude??? Praise you, Jesus. Your plan is greater than mine. Your will be done, Heavenly Father.

You are doing a great work in me. If all I will ever be is what I am now. If all I will ever be able to do is make it by and pray every night on this page for men till the day I come home to you Dad? Then so be it.

Dad, I want the men on this page now and the future men coming to this page to see what happens when we don't treat our blessing, our wives, your daughters the way we should. Allow them to come to this page sooner call them to come to this group sooner. So that they can see how to avoid the destruction and pain I have caused myself and your daughter.

Help me tonight to forgive myself for what I have done Dad.

In Jesus' name, I pray.

Amen."

Just vomiting out my heart, like I did most nights.

"Heavenly Father I come to you tonight exhausted and drained, but not finished and not giving up. Yes, Dad, I have my down moments when I feel like I can't take anymore. But something in me says "One more time Eddie, you got this!! It's not over, this just started!" That has to be You talking to me Dad. So here I am yet again, not giving up, not quoting, not procrastinating.

So, I stand firm in my faith in You Dad. I stand in the gap for my brothers on this page. I'm not backing down Dad. I will not submit to the enemy. Dad, I can't do that I can't let my family down; I can't let You down. You are my creator; you are my Father. You are MY Shepard. You will never let me down so why would I quit on You. Something is going to turn. Something is going to change. Something is going to get better. I don't care how long it takes Dad I will pray to You every day and every night.

Father God, I pray for my brothers. I pray that you help us all become stronger and more focused on what you need us to focus on. I'm sick of seeing the enemy winning these battles Dad. I'm sick of seeing all this pain and feeling all of this pain that he is causing. Help us heal quickly so that we can get back on the battleground. I pray that during these difficult times You speak to my brothers and me who are hurting in a way that we can tell it's You and only You. Please, Father, restore us. We have failed time and

*time again by trying to do things our way. I
more than most. I fight everything including
You and Your will.*

*I no longer want to waste my life fighting
you Dad. Please help me be good with Your
will. Make Your will mine. Help me be ok
with the way things have gone and will go.
Help me be the man you need me to be.*

I pray this for my brothers here tonight.

*I pray for her tonight dad. I pray that she has
a beautiful night's sleep. I pray that
tomorrow is the best day of her life because
tomorrow you speak to her and comfort her.
I pray you strengthen her self-esteem and
her confidence.*

*I pray all of this in your holy name Jesus.
Amen."*

Still searching for forgiveness.

*"Heavenly Father I pray tonight asking for
forgiveness. You blessed me with some
amazing time with my baby girl. You blessed
me with the fact that my baby girl wanted to
spend time with Bri tonight and they did. I
am asking for forgiveness Dad. Because I am
honestly jealous because I can't have time
with Bri. How childish of me Dad... I am sorry
I should be glorifying you for this moment.
For the fact that my baby girl spent the
majority of the day with me, for the fact that*

my baby girl is helping me, for the fact that she is going to be coming over this weekend and spending the night with us Friday and Saturday. Why am I like this Dad? Why can I not sit in these moments even longer? Dad I know I am being selfish, and I have been working hard on not being that way. But Dad please, I want Bri back so bad. I long to be able to hold her hand. Take her out for coffee, dinner, a movie, Barns and Noble, for a walk in the park. Ugh, I need to pull my big boy underwear up I know.

I know Sydney told me today that she feels like I have to focus on some things in my life and grow in those areas so I can be stronger in this area with Bri. She told me I need to see myself the others see me... Strong, able, loving, secure... I can't do that right now. For some reason Dad I feel like I am slipping back into my emotional cesspool. No more pity parties Dad... I promised myself this and I can't even keep that promise how am I going to be able to do anything to get Bri back if I can't even keep a promise to myself?

I'm trying to shack this crap off Dad. So, because I feel like this right now in this moment, I am Running to you Dad. I need that kick in the butt you so loving giving me. I am not looking for sympathy at all. I am coming to you because I have to. Because I want to.

Dad, I pray tonight that you help my brothers tonight with their situations. Help us all with our sins, past, present, and future.

I pray you give me knowledge Dad. That is all I am really asking for.

In Jesus' name, I pray. Amen."

Even in my pain and self-pity, I would pray for Bri. Wife or not I prayed for her all the time.

"Heavenly Father I pray to you this evening with a humbled heart. Dad, I come to you seeking you and your face. Not your hands for the blessing and handouts. I'm seeking your face tonight because I want to know you better. I want to understand your word better. I want to hear from you.

Dad I know there are things you need and want me to do, steps I need to take. I think I am heading in the right direction, but I could use a little something to let me know. Some sort of confirmation. That's why I want to hear from you.

I ask that you protect Bri tonight. I ask that you pull her closer to you Dad. I ask that you speak to her parents so that they can forgive me for hurting their baby girl.

Dad, I know that you have forgiven me, and I know I am working on forgiving myself.

Thank you for helping me in this area of my life.

I also pray tonight for my brothers and their situations. I know they are praying for their marriages and relationships to be restored and I pray that same prayer for them. I pray that you help guide each of us to you tonight Dad.

I pray this in your holy name Jesus. Amen."

I knew I needed to give up control but was having issues leaving it all at the cross.

"Heavenly Father I pray to you right now asking for you to take over my life and the lives of my brothers here on this page. Dad, I y'all a good game here on this page, but You know the truth about me. Dad I'm filled with anger and worry, anxiety and depression, fear and everything else I shouldn't be. I'm so full of these things I don't have more room for you. We need to learn to create capacity for you to fill us up.

Lord, I want to be filled with you and you light. My life is yours Dad. I need you to take over and I am willing to submit to you and your will. Help me see the joy, and the blessings you are giving me every day.

Dad, I want to keep living. Living every day not just existing. Use me, Dad. Use me daily.

237

*Restore me, change me into the man you
need me to be.*

Please, Dad, do this for my brothers today.

In Jesus' name, I pray. Amen."

This night was not a good night for me. Thoughts were creeping in my head that had not been there in years.

" Heavenly Father this time of year sucks for some of us. Brokenness and emptiness of our homes reminds us of so many mistakes we can't go back and erase. Separation from loved ones reminds us of our mistakes and helps breed more pain. Thoughts may start creeping into some people's heads. So, Dad, I pray till I can't pray anymore that you be with my brothers tonight and tomorrow. Fill them with so much joy and happiness that those types of thoughts and emotions and feelings have no room. I'm praying this while I shake off my emotions. I pray this for my brothers as well as me Dad.

I feel thoughts creeping in and I rebuke them in the name of Jesus Christ. Help us focus on you and your love Dad. I pray for peace and joy for my brother's Dad.

Ugh, I am back to a low point Dad. I thought I was past this crap. I understand grieving but this has to stop. I need you Dad. I need you to help me get past this point. I need a breakthrough. I'm fighting Dad. I am trying everything I can to do what you need me to do. I'm not sure if I am doing it or not.

So many questions, and emotions all at once. You have surrounded me with people time and time again. Yet I feel alone. You are with me, but I feel alone. Why can't I get through this now?

One more day, one more step forward. Day by day. I will push forward. God, it hurts. It's coming in waves again and I'm standing firm in my faith that you will help me through this as well as my brothers.

I'm not going to give up. That's too damn easy. I'm not weak. I'm not pathetic. I am worthy and I am loved. And I am forgiven.

I declare this in your holy name Jesus.

Amen"

"Heavenly Father I pray to you tonight just trying to seek you more. You know my wants and needs Dad. You know my pain and my joy. You know everything about me. I can't be fake with you Dad.

I know you have forgiven me for everything. I'm still working on forgiving myself for things. But I'm having trouble. It seems as I forgive myself for something but then something else pops up. It gets overwhelming so I seek you Dad. Help me, please. I want to move forward I need to move forward. I need your help to heal. I need your help to stay focused on changing and growing.

I'm praying for every man on this page too dad. That you help my brothers stay focused on you Dad. We could use some wins Dad. We need you Dad. I'm asking you tonight Dad to bring my brothers and their brides back together. Please heal their marriages.

Dad, I pray for her tonight. I miss her dad. I have no clue if she misses me. But I miss her so much. I wish I could tell her myself. Dad can you speak to her and let know. I don't know what else to do but to ask you to bless her and protect her Dad. Bless her socks off Dad.

I pray all this in Jesus' holy name. Amen."

Ok, so yeah, I get it, not the best to cuss at God when praying, but he knew what was in my thoughts and on my heart.

"Heavenly Father I pray to you tonight. I need you Dad. I need you now more than ever. Every day I feel the need for you to grow more and more. While I feel alone, I know I am not. While I feel weak, I know you give me strength. It is such an odd feeling Dad. It's like a tug of war. That tug to run to you vs the tug to just say "f@$* it, go do

*what I want and forget about everything".
But my drive to get closer to you I feel is
winning every time.*

*Thank you, Jesus, for this. It is crazy how I
want to give up but can't. Fear running
through my body but feeling safe at the
same time. Tired but have the ability to keep
moving forward in things.*

*I'm ready to move forward Dad. I am ready
to take the next step. Let's do this Dad. One
step at a time I ask that you be here with me
like you have been for years.*

*Dad, I pray for the restoration of the
marriages on this page. I ask that you smack
the devil away like a fly. Allow us to grow
faster and allow our wives to see our
changes and allow wounds to heal. Dad, I
pray our wives, your daughters open up to
us.*

*I pray for Bri tonight Dad. Help her see how
amazing she truly is.*

In Jesus' name, I pray. Amen."

Feeling inadequate in this one.

*"Heavenly Father I pray to you tonight just
looking for you to direct me and guide me.
Father, I come to you because I need you and
want you in my life. Dad, I love you. I have a
long journey ahead of me. I don't know*

where to turn at times, so I rely on you and you alone to guide me in the right direction.

I trust you Dad. I have faith that you have not forsaken me and my family. I know you love; I don't understand how or why but you do and that is enough.

I don't want to hold anything back from you. How can you know my every thought? Yet there are times Dad when I try to hide things from you. I don't like how my choices have molded my life into what it has been. But I'm thankful for everything that has happened to me. While a lot of it hurt and still does, I will make it because I have you.

Dad, I thank you for the victories you have had with my brothers on this page. I'm thankful for the friends that have been reaching out to me recently. Although I don't understand why you keep bringing me people that are depressed or going through so much pain. I feel like I have nothing to give them, except You. But I don't know what to do, how to do it. I don't know what to say to them or how to say it.

So, Dad all I can do is pray for them. For my brothers on this page, I pray you continue to do a great work in them.

For my friends that have started hitting me up about their marriage issues, depression, suicidal thoughts, etc. I pray for them Dad. I

*pray you heal us all and restore us to the
men you need and want us to be.*

*Dad, we need to submit everything to You
right now. So here I am. I submit everything
to you Dad. Without you Dad, I will not make
it.*

*I thank you for being willing to take all my
issues and trash and make something
amazing one day. All the glory to you God.*

*I pray for my family and the families on this
page. Restore God.*

*I pray for her tonight Dad. Again, I ask that
you let her know I love her and wish her the
best. Protect her and talk to her. Guide her
down the path you need her to be on.*

In Jesus' name, I pray. Amen."

Sometimes you need to pray for others.

*"Heavenly Father I pray tonight for all my
brothers and their families on this page. I
pray for the restoration of their marriages. I
pray for healing for both the men and the
women, the children, and the extended
families. Dad, please give us the ability and
willingness to start changing into the people
you need us to be.*

*Dad beyond the broken relationships that
are part of this page I pray for the sick family*

members tonight. I pray that you heal the mental sickness, the physical sickness that is causing stress for everyone involved.

Dad I am asking you to shower us with your favor. We glorify you Dad regardless, but I do ask that you please reunite us with our families and wives. Restore the covenants that we have with you. Dad so many men on this page have so many people watching. Use us to show the world who you are and how you take care of your children. We are your children and we have not done right but you love us and take care of us.

Dad, I pray for her tonight. Let her know she will be ok. Let her know how much she is loved and valued by you and many others. Protect her emotional well-being from those attacking it.

Dad, I know this is selfish, but I ask, if you're willing, please bring her back closer to me sooner rather than later. Straighten me to make deep lasting changes to show her I am sorry, that I adore her, that I am safe, that I am not the abusive person she has labeled me as. I didn't know what I was doing. I never meant to hurt your daughter Dad. I never meant to be controlling. I am sorry Dad. I know you know this and have forgiven me. But can you please help me forgive myself for what I have done to her? Can you help her forgive me?

If you're will Dad can I have a second chance with her as my bride and mother of my two older kids?

I pray this in your heavenly name Jesus. Amen."

Feeling weak, again. So, I run to prayer.

"Heavenly Father I pray to you tonight giving you thanks for today. Giving you all the glory. Dad tonight I want to get real with you. I want to pour it all out. I want to drain everything I have into this prayer to you for my brothers and myself.

Lord, we entered into a covenant with you the day we said, "I do". Lord that covalent should have been protected by us but we failed. Dad, I failed you and I failed my bride your daughter.

Now, Dad, I understand you forgive us for this. You saw it coming. You see it all before we do it. We didn't listen to You Dad. We didn't follow Your instructions. So here we are now Dad. We have made a mess of your plan for us and so here we are asking you to fix it. But we need faith, we need to have hope, we need to believe with all of our being Dad that you have this, and you can and will correct our mistakes and bring order to our lives.

*So, Dad tonight, as weak as my faith and belief and hope maybe, or as strong as it is, I am stating that **you got this**. That you will correct me if I would just drop fighting you and your plan. I have to believe that Bro was a gift from you. A blessing from you Dad. You set that meeting up and I followed your guidance. I didn't want a relationship or a wife at that time. She helped correct a lot of my wrong thoughts. She brought me to you Dad. She showed my children who you are. She showed my babies what a loving mother is. She protected them as if they were her own. Only you could have or Orchestrated such unconditional love Dad.*

So tonight dad I am here standing as firm as I possibly can stating I believe and know you will correct all of this. You and only You dad will correct us and our wrongs. Dad, I believe that this suffering we are going through is to bring us closer to you. Dad, we love you and trust you. I believe that my wife will open back up to me. So that I Amy date you're daughter again. Dad, I believe you are restoring my marriage with Bri. I claim this victory tonight in your holy name Jesus.

Dad, I have a crush on your daughter. I would like your permission to date your daughter again.

I ask this same thing for my brothers on this page. Please allow us to date and court your daughters like we once did. Just better this time. More focused on you Dad. I am changing Dad. I am growing. I will be a better man for her and You.

I claim victory over the enemy. I claim victory over any demonic oppression holding my wife or my family back. Any that are ripping these families apart. No more Dad.

I pray this in your holy name Jesus. Amen."

He gives me strength when I need it.

"Heavenly Father. I pray to you tonight thanking you for today. Dad, as always you helped me make it through. I don't know what everyone on the page is feeling or going through Dad, but you do. Help them, Father. Guide them.

As for me Dad. I'm tired. I would like a break. I could use some deep refreshing rest. I would like if you're willing, a second chance with Bri.

I pray for her tonight. Keep her safe as she moves out of her parents' place this coming weekend.

In Jesus' holy name I pray. Amen."

Just a simple Christmas day prayer for my brothers who were not with their family.

"Heavenly Father thank you for today. Another day we can celebrate You and your glory. Another day for us to try to work on us. Another day to draw closer to you.

While others are spending time with family and some of us are not it is ok. Maybe it is because you need us to have that downtime. Time for me to sit down and focus on you and our relationship.

Thank you for the past Christmas with family and kids running around. But today Dad I'm just sitting here with you. Working on me and you. No screaming, no family drama, no running here and there. Just You and me. Thank.

I pray that you fill my brother's hearts with joy today regardless of their situations. I pray that you show them each and every opportunity with their wives and families. I pray that you give them the words to say or text that will help move them forward and closer to restoration. Bless them, Dad.

I pray this in your holy name Jesus. Amen."

I started seeking wisdom.

"Dad, it's me again. I'm here again to pray again for my brothers and myself. I am tired, at times I feel like I don't have another step in me. I know some of my brothers feel this too. But I am not here for pity, I am here to

say thank you for giving me the energy to take that next step. I strength to take that next step. Dad, I don't know what else to say but thank you, thank you, Dad, for everything. Thank you for all the people that are coming to me with marital problems, like I have answers. Like I can help them. Good night Dad look at my life. What do I have to offer them? Well, that answer is my prayers and you. That's all I have to offer my friends and my brothers. I am pouring out everything I have here, every day. I try not to hold back. When I am tired, I try to remember to come to you. When I don't, I fall, when I do you carry me.

Your love is sufficient Dad. Your love is really all we need. We want the love of our wives, of our children... but we don't need it. We long for it, but Dad I don't need it. I am solid if it is just You and me.

I am still fighting the enemy on my brother's behalf, and my own. I am still fighting for your daughter's love; I am still fighting for her attention. Why? Cause you blessed me with her. She was my blessing from you. She was the light you put in my life to draw me to You, and I wasted it. Yet You keep blessing me. And I thank you for that.

Dad, I again pray for wisdom. That is all I want. I have your love; I have your forgiveness. I have You. I lack wisdom, so please Dad if you're willing, please bless me with wisdom.

In Jesus Holy Name I pray. Amen."

"Heavenly Father I come to you night with a humble heart. I pray for my brothers tonight. I have not looked at all the posts Dad, but I know there are broken hearts, tired souls, and pain. I pray for each and every man on this page. I pray blessing of peace, healing, relief, and love for them all.

Dad, you are doing something great in each and every one of us. I pray thanking you for never giving up on us even when we turn our eyes away from you and mess things up for ourselves. You are always there with us and you always help us get back on the right path. Thank you, Dad.

I pray tonight for all the wives, girlfriends, ex-wives, and relationships represented on this page. I pray that you protect your daughters. Speak to them and call them back to you. Call us men back to you as well.

In Jesus' holy name I pray. Amen."

Feeling froggy in this one. Like I was a fighter like I could go the distance. Getting ready for battle so to speak.

"Heavenly Father thank you for today. While I am tired and feel like I have no more energy I know you will be with me and hold me up so I can keep moving forward. I'm not giving up Dad I am admitting I need your help in this situation.

Dad, I know there are some of my brothers feeling the same way and need you to help them up as well, so I am praying not just for me but for them as well. I pray for restoration for each of us tonight. I am claiming victory tonight in our situations, Dad. Dad give us all the strength to go another day. Pushing forward and focusing on You. Like my friend said to me tonight. You must have something amazing for me and brothers or the enamel would not be coming at us the way he is.

Dad, I pray for my dad tonight as well. He is letting himself go. He is not doing the things he needs to in order to keep himself going. I know he wants to be with You and mom really bad. But letting himself go the way he is and not taking care of himself is hurting me and my kids. Dad talk to him. Help him see that he needs to take care of himself. His seizure lasting longer than any of the other ones have. This tells me he is not doing what the doctors told him. Please heal him, Dad.

Dad, I'm ready for another round. I'm a fighter and not a quitter. So, let's do this.

Ring that bell step into the cage with me and let's get this done Dad. I'm ready.

I pray for her tonight again dad. I pray that you be with her tonight. She seems ok on the outside but the texts I get from her tell me she is dealing with things. I want to help her, but I don't know how to. Give me the wisdom and discernment to be able to help her where and when You want and need me to.

In Jesus Holy name I pray. Amen."

Chapter 20

From Hate to Love

C hristmas passed, new years passed, back to work and teaching the kids class, working on my purple belt, working on me. I got back to listening to my sleep meditation videos at night to try and help me sleep. Words of affirmation, calming videos reading scripture to me at night. It was helping me sleep a bit, no nightmares. I started dreaming again, well, having dreams, that is. Beautiful happy dreams. It may not seem like much to you, but for me it was great.

My baby girl was back from Australia and wanted to come to visit us. We went to lunch and just laughed and talked. Heard all about her trip, she showed me pictures she took, we talked about how when she was younger her mom and I took them to those places. She talked to me about how she was able to decompress and reflect on a lot of what had happened, and what she had said to me about things.

I asked if she wanted to see the apartment and she excitedly said yes.

She told me that she loved that apartment, but I need to decorate it, and how she was going to come over and help.

She said, *"Would it be ok if I start coming over and spending the weekend with you?"*

"Of course, it is."

"Ok, and I know I have not been going to church and all that. Have you?"

"No, I have not been going regularly."

"You need that daddy, and I want to start going with you. Can we go back to Momentum together?"

Here it comes again, that fear, that pain in the chest. What the hell is going on? This is a happy moment, why is this happening now? Not again, no I am going to fight this. I am going to push this back.

"Daddy, are you ok? You are shaking."

"I got his baby girl."

"We got this. Now breathe with me. Count to 10 with me. We got this, you and me."

This time it went away faster. I told I was so sorry for being so weak again, that I am trying everything I can to get my emotions under control it is just hard for me for some reason. I admitted to my daughter that I hate myself, and I hate what I had become. Then she hit me with some amazing words.

"Daddy you are stronger than you know. You don't see you the way that I see you. You have always been there when we need you. Why can't you see yourself the way that we do? Why do you hate yourself so much? You are an amazing dad. You almost destroyed your life trying to give Luke and me what we wanted, no matter how man times we changed that on you. Please see how amazing you are. Please see yourself through other people's eyes. Because that is who you are. I am going to help you learn how to love yourself."

She was right, I had spent all my life listening to all the negative things people would say to me about me while ignoring all the positive things people said to me and about me. This was another new start for me, another chance to reset.

I wish I could tell you all that from that moment on I loved myself, but that is not that case. Like most things in my life, I am having to work overtime to do this. I find myself slip here and there. I must be very intentional about this. When I feel myself slipping, I remind myself of what she told me. I write things down now that I like about myself. I work daily on this task. My list is growing minute by minute.

That evening when I took her home, I asked her about my jokes. She told me that while she finds my jokes funny, it does concern her that one day I might not be joking. She said that she brushes it off, but at times she worries about me. I have since promised both my kids that my dark jokes would stop.

I am a good dad. I am a good man. I am not a monster. I am getting better.

As of today, we have not been able to match our schedules for her to come over and help decorate, but we talk more. I still text her, and I still get my *"hope yours is better"* text from her. Also, it has only been about two weeks since this all happened so it's not like I have gone months without seeing her.

One day I get a text from my sister-in-law, my brother's wife. She needed to talk to me about my dad. Dad was in the hospital, she found him passed out in his motorhome. Apparently, he was having complications with his MS and his health overall.

Out of everything good comes something bad, and out of everything bad comes something good. This bad news of my dad brought on the restoration of my relationship with my brother and sister-in-law. Thank you, Jesus!

She would update me daily on my dad. We would talk about all the shit we were all told about each other. Regarding my dad, from I was being told, he was having seizures again. This was causing him to pass out. More results came in, the doctors were saying that dad had a stroke. Maybe two. Dad was telling the doctors that he had a stroke years ago, but he was fine. Too many conflicting stories. I was told no strokes, seizures had not happened for a long time. Well, what we were all finding out was this was not the whole truth.

I found out that on his way up to Virginia to visit he messed his motor home up a bit, there were new dents along the side of it. I was also told that he wrecked my brother's truck one day, and my sister in-law's car. Three accidents in one month. This was not good at all.

He was starting to get mad at the doctors for not being able to leave the hospital when he wanted. I get it, I hate hospitals myself, but they are there for a reason.

Things were being said about me and my family, at the same time things were said about my brother and his family when my dad was down here with me. Lots of drama, misunderstandings, lack of communication, etcetera. The three of us decided to band together and stop listening to the "he said, she said" bullshit.

Dad needed help, and I hate to say it, but I could not help. He was better off with my brother and his wife. He needed to get healthy and be taken care of some until he was better. My mental and emotional state made me the back up plan so to speak. I was there to support them. I just had to bow out and say I can't. I need to work on me and get my crap together. This is the first time in my life I did not jump into an issue saying, "I got this, I can help." Honestly, it felt great saying "no".

Remember you must take care of yourself, because if you are not healthy how can you help others? Common sense, right? Not for some of us.

F.M.L

Chapter 21

Anybody Have a Time Machine?

I have been asked many times throughout my life "If you could go back and redo anything in your life, what would it be?" I have always said I would change nothing because it is what has made me who I am today. Looking back, I would like to change my answer. There are so many things that I would like to go back in time and redo or change.

This list of things I would like to change could be a book all on its own I bet. I understand that I cannot go back in time, but if I could, I would. All I can do at this point is reflect, find the errors I made, the areas I would love to change in the past, and make sure that I make the changes in me now so I never make those choices that way again.

But if I could go back in time, I would not have to go back that far.

That's right I would not go back to my first marriage to fix anything there, I would not go back to high school and change things there. Nope, not at all. I would not even go back to my childhood to change anything there. Why not? Because I am good with where those choices got me up to a point in my life.

I would go back just a few years, back to the day I went to Lifetime Fitness to talk with Bri. That's my point I would go back to. What would I do differently you ask? Hell, everything?

So, let's take this trip back in time. Not to have a pity party, not to torture me. No, but maybe to help someone who has done the same things I have or is making the same mistakes I did. Maybe this will help you correct things that you are doing right now. Maybe you can save your relationship from disaster.

Let's do this in little steps.

If I could go back to some points in my past I would for sure go back to July 5th, 2019 and not have gone to the house to see what I could find. I would not have broken even more trust with Bri that night by looking at her phone. I would have trusted that she needed space and time to think. I would go back to July 3rd and not accused her of having an affair. I would have trusted that she loved me and was just hurt by me and my actions. I would not have had too much to drink that Saturday night, I would have been open and honest and talked to her that day about how I was feeling. I would have communicated with her to see how she was doing and asked how we could start fixing things.

I would have closed the gym every night at 7:00 PM and gone home and noticed what she needed, and just helped take care of dinner, the cleaning, and little dude. I would never have gone to sleep on the couch or in the guest room. I would have held her hand more often. I would have always sat next to her on the couch instead of telling her to come to sit next to me. I would have gone to Florida with her, the gym didn't need me I could have closed it and gone on a vacation with my wife.

When she first talked about going to counseling, I would have jumped on that with her, for me and for us. I would not have overextended us financially in a rental house. I would have gotten a job after being laid off and we would not have just lived off the inheritance. I would have not opened the gym but started it off as a martial arts school and worked it after I got off work.

I would have made it known that I respected the fact that I valued her as a "housewife" and stay at home mom. I would have made it 100% clear that is just as valuable if not more than what I was doing. I would not have guilted her by complaining about how I worked and brought in the money to pay the bills.

I would never, ever, have said: *"what do you want me to do, cut my wrists and bleed my body dry for you all?"* I would have included her in a lot more of the financial decisions instead of just telling her *"I got it."* I would have asked her more loving questions to understand where she was coming from in a lot of situations. I would never have gotten into the arguments I got into with her family, I would have tried to help her calm down without telling her to calm down. I would have allowed her to vent, while I listened, without coming up with "solutions". I would have done a better job providing financial security for her and the kids. I would have made it known to her that I was not putting the kids above her.

I would have jumped for joy when she told me she was pregnant. I would have allowed the joy to flow out of me instead of the fear as failing father. I would have kissed her more. God, I would have held her hand all damn day long and never let go until she did. I would have cooked dinner to allow her to relax.

I would have listened to her music more often, which means I would have listened to Country music. I would have set up more date nights with her. I would have been there for her emotionally. I would not have laughed when she would make fun of her childhood pictures, making her feel like I was making fun of how she looked as well. I would have made it clear how amazing and beautiful she was, not just physically but spiritually, internally. I would have focused more on her and her wants and needs instead of assuming I knew what she wanted and was feeling.

I would never have stopped going to the park with her for walks on the weekends. I would have worked so fucking hard to have a good relationship with her family, her mom, and dad. I would never have cussed them out the way I did. I would never have allowed my frustration to bleed out of me with the insults and rude comments about them. I would have fostered an environment where we as a couple could have set healthy boundaries with her family instead of trying to "be the man" and strong-arm them.

We would have had a joint account the second we got married so that she never felt like she was having to ask for permission to spend money.

I would have properly proposed to her, on my knee, without my stupid joke. I would never complain about how much she was on her phone and posting on social media. I would have taken more pictures of and with her and posted them myself. I would not have moved in with her, because I knew her parents disagreed with that and us doing that caused a lot of stress between us, and her parents.

God, I would have watched *The Notebook* and *Titanic* and any other romance movie more often without complaining. I would have allowed her to help. I would have told her *"I love you, and I am in love with you"* the second I knew I was instead of waiting for a couple of weeks. I would have stopped smoking the second she asked me to instead of trying to hide it from her. I would have stayed in those nights she wanted to just spend time with me, instead of making her go out and hang with people. I would have done more of what she wanted. I would have set better boundaries with my ex so that she could not have caused all the negativity in our lives. I would have spent more quality time with her, listening instead of talking. Hearing what she had to say, her thoughts, hopes, dreams, desires. I would have been a leader and not a boss.

Again, I would hold her hand more, from the beginning, I would have held her hand while walking, while driving, while sitting on the couch, while laying bed sleeping. I would have made time for her more often.

These are just a few things I would change if I could go back in time and change things. I believe with every ounce of my being, that I would have at least be in counseling working on my marriage with Bri if I had done these things listed above. I would not be writing this book about two divorces. This story would be different for sure.

Guys, if you are doing anything like what I have done to Bri, I beg you to stop, I beg you to go seek help right now. Stop reading this and get your ass in a counseling group. Unless you want to be in my shoes, then keep fucking things up, just like I did.

I got a second chance at a happy life, and family. God blessed me with a woman who did not have to step up and be a mom to kids that were not hers, but Bri did. She did not have to put up with all my issues and bullshit, but God damn she did. Like a mother fucking champ, she stepped the fuck up, and I fucked it up.

Bri, I am so sorry for everything. If I had the chance to it all over again, I would jump on that. I would show you that I can be trusted, I would not hurt you, I can be a good husband. That you are valued by me, your thoughts and opinions are valuable and needed in my life. I pray you forgive me for the horrible things I did to you and the way I made you feel. I never meant to do this to you. I pray that you find happiness. You are the strongest, smartest, funniest woman I know. You are the complete package. I should have cherished you more. I am grateful God pulled us together for those 8 years. They were the best 8 years of my life so far. I know I failed you as a husband, I am sorry!

Chapter 22

Baby Girl, Bubba, Little, Support

I am moving forward with my life and I could not be doing it without my support group. Still have a lot of growing to do, changes to make. I am learning to love myself in a humble way. I know that I am not that fucking special. This story might be nothing compared to your story, it might be a warning to you, might give some hope, inspire you to make some changes in your life. Hell, maybe it can be a road map to avoid destruction? I am just hoping that this helps someone.

So, who is my support group? Well, my baby girl (Sydney), Bubba (Lucas), my little (Landon). Amy Hill, my Life Coach. Brother Al, the 1300 plus men on Amy's Facebook page *"Building Powerful Marriages for Christian Men"*. My Jiu-Jitsu family. My brother and sister-in-law, my friends. My Creator and Heavenly Father God, my savior Jesus.

You need to find a support group for sure but keep your circle tight, small even. Don't be a friend whore like me.

Also, learn to set healthy boundaries with people, you don't always have to say yes like me. It is ok to say no, it is healthy as a matter of fact.

I am learning that I don't owe anyone an explanation of what is going on in my life. This means I don't have to tell people every damn thing going on. They don't need to know all the little details, ironic that I am pouring all this stuff out in a book, right?

Find things that make you happy, for me it is time with my kids, my BJJ, music.

I love listening to music and dancing around the apartment with my little dude. Listening to him sing the songs wrong is the highlight of my day.

On that note, I have to say that music helps me out so much. It can bring back some of the best moments of my life. Songs that helped me through rough times, my suicidal past, and the writing of this book.

My daughter told me once that I need to make a playlist. I needed to find new music to listen to. I did just that, most of the time though I just go to YouTube and search a band and let it roll. But here are some of the bands and artists I listen to while I write this book, or if I am chilling out, dancing with my little dude.

- Cold
- Machine Gun Kelly
- Yungblud
- Staind
- Korn

- Tool
- A Day to Remember (Degenerates and Rescue Me are two of the songs little and I dance to)
- Cartel
- Mudvayne
- Elevation Worship
- Hillsong United
- Puddle of Mudd
- Alice in Chains
- Anything Dubstep… And so much more.

Currently, while writing this book, my playlist is as follows:

- MGK
  - 27
  - I Think I'm Okay
  - Candy
  - 5:3666
  - Raise the Flag
  - Dopeman
  - Swing Life Away
  - Rehab
  - Waste Love
  - Let You Go
  - Why Are You Here
- Yungblud
  - Original Me
  - 11 Minutes
  - Medication
- Cold
  - Bleed
  - Wasted Years

- o Gone Away
- o Suffocate
- o End of the World
- o A Letter to God

For some reason, this music helps me remember and keeps me calm while running through the torment I have caused in my life and other peoples. Healthy or not this helps me to create a road map of my past and has helped me get out of the mental fog I have been in recently.

I have even started to listen to some country music. By reading all of this I am sure you have figured out that I am not poetic or good with words. So, I relate to music like a teenager, a 41-year-old teenager. Sometimes in my darkest moments, I find that dark depressing music lifts me up. It takes me to a place where I can see that while I have a lot of shitty moments in life, others have it much worse than me. I can see or hear other people's pain and it opens my eyes to how good I have it.

Some say I have been through hell and back. I guess it is all relative right. While I sit back and see other people going through hell and I think *"fuck I could not handle all that"* there have been people that think that same of me and what I have and am going through.

Even while writing this book, areas of my life are still filling up with issues. My dad has been having those seizures, I guess he has had a mini-stroke or two. My brother might have cancer. My business is not exactly taking care of itself. Bills are coming in faster than the money is. But God has a plan for me. What is that plan? I do not know, but there is a plan. It is not a plan to destroy me, it is not that he has forsaken me. No, I have done that to myself. He loves me, he loves you too. I don't care if you believe in Him or not, He still loves you.

At this point I start moving forward, again, rebuilding my life, my self-esteem, and my future. I cannot go back in time to undo the hurt I have done, so I can only pick up all the pieces and start rebuilding. Maybe some people will see the changes I am making and be willing to give me another chance, maybe they won't. I cannot focus on that, I can only focus on the things I have "control" of. Like my actions, my words, my thoughts, and my reactions to things.

> *To all of you in my life who have been there*
> *for me through all this shit. Thank you.*
> *Thank you for the love, the support, the*
> *prayer, good vibes, and ears that listened,*
> *the shoulders to cry on. The phone calls*
> *calling me out when I have been a little*
> *bitch. Much love to you all.*

Chapter 23

F.M.L.

That acronym right there. Man, I remember eight years ago being in a dramatic stage and posting that on my Facebook page. Little did I know that posting *"Fuck my life"* would have brought me the most amazing woman in my life and my third child, very dramatic I know. As well as so much pain, and growth. I have been running those three simple letters through my head over, and over, again in my head. The crazy thing is even the meaning of those letters changed in my head. It went from *"Fuck My Life"* to *"Forgive me, Lord"*. I have cried those words out so many times, monthly, weekly, and daily.

I know I am forgiven, not that this gives me a license to go do whatever I want. Nope, not that at all. I am forgiven, now I must change and grow more. This means more pain, letting go of old habits that I was comfortable with.

I used to burn myself with lighters, just to see if I could take the pain. I love getting tattoos to see how long I can take the pain, plus telling a story of my life. If you think about it, as much as I love pain, you would think I would enjoy this. It is not fun, but it is necessary. I was told once, and have no clue if this true or not, that as a snake grows it must shed its skin. That process is not comfortable for them. Think about it. If we had to shed our skin the same way, how painful would that be? Would we want to go through that? Your skin being ripped off your body, exposing new fresh skin. It does not sound pleasant to me.

I remember when all this stuff went down, I would be in class, stuck in a submission. I would allow my training partner to hold on to that submission to see how much pain I could handle, also in a lot of cases I could not get out of it, regardless I would allow the pain to get so bad that I had to tap out or something was going to break. The chokeholds, yup that's right, I would sit there hoping that I would blackout. *Snap, nap, or tap.* Not that I am some badass, no way. I would do that to start feeling something besides that regret and emotional pain I was going through. I wanted to feel anything besides that. This is not healthy, it is not smart to sit there and almost pass out or have an arm break, but I would see how far I could go before having to submit.

Writing this book has been painful. Reliving all the mistakes I made, the pain I caused to the people I loved the most. I look at it was a way to peel the dead skin off so that I can grow more. This process has been very cathartic for me. But I have found for me, that learning to put up with the pain and learning when to tap out, has been an amazing journey. I am learning to be comfortable in uncomfortable positions I guess you could say. Then using the techniques, I have learned in group to get myself out of those situations or positions so that I can advance and grow.

I am sure some of you might be wondering what the point is of this book. Honestly, I have no clue. Maybe this is just me wiring it all down like a teenage girl and her diary. Maye it is me pointing it all out there, again, as a road map of what not to do in your life and relationship. Maybe it is to try and show you that no matter what you are going through in life, you can still go another day.

I found hope through Christ through this process. I can look back and see so many points in my life where God showed up and saved me from something horrible. At the same time, I can see where is sat back and was like *"Dude, Eddie, don't do that. I mean if you want to do that go for it. I am trying to tell you no, but you are wanting to do it. I will be here when you are ready to get back on track."* I can see those points in my life. I can see that no matter how many times He says go right, and I go left, He is still there with me. If you believe in God, just know He is there waiting for you to turn to him for everything. If you don't believe in Him, that's coo, He still loves you and He is still waiting for you to turn to Him.

All you need to do is start talking to Him, then listen. He will talk to you.

A few questions I would love to hear the answer from him on is this. *Why do men wait so fucking long to get help? Why do we not seek professional help sooner? Why did I wait so long to seek help for myself and my relationship? Why did I wait till she was done?*

So, guys, if you are in a relationship, and you think it might be going downhill. Stop what you are doing and get some help now. I think I may have stated this already, but I am just trying to be real with you. She is worth it, regardless of what you are going through as a couple, she is worth it. I don't care if "she is the problem", she is worth it. Be the leader, don't blame her, look deep inside to find what you are doing wrong. Nothing is ever 100% one-sided. We all have our part in messing things up. There are almost always signs that things need to change, that things are not headed in the right direction.

Even if you are not a Christ-follower, read this and apply it to your marriage or relationship.

Psalm 23 (ESV) English Standard Version.

> *"The Lord is my shepherd, I lack nothing. He makes me lie down in green pastures, he leads me beside quiet waters, he refreshes my soul. He guides me along the right paths for his name's sake. Even though I walk through the darkest valley, I will fear no evil, for you are with me; your rod and your staff, they comfort me. You prepare a table before me in the presence of my enemies. You anoint my head with oil; my cup overflows. Surely your goodness and love will follow me*

all the days of my life, and I will dwell in the
house of the Lord forever."

Imagine if your wife, girlfriend, significant other through this of you. Man, that would be amazing, wouldn't it? Think about if they feared nothing because of you and your loving actions towards them. Imagine if they were so comfortable and relaxed because of you.

At this point in my life, I long for my kids to feel this way about me. I feel this way about my relationship with God. I just want to reflect this in my life and my relationships.

I have hurt a lot of people over my 41 years of life. Mainly the people closest to me. I have pushed them away in moments of self-pity and depression. Looking back at my life I see where I made a lot of mistakes, and truly wish I could go back and change things, or at least know that they have accepted my apologies. I would give anything to be able to wipe those words, actions, and times out of their memory.

The thing is we can't go back in time. We can only work on making the changes now. You need to recognize what it is you are doing wrong and find the proper ways to make healthy changes. Work on it daily. Set goals, I use Amy Hill's SMART ACTION plan to set my goals.

S – Specific
M – Measurable
A – Attainable
R – Relevant
T – Time-specific

A – Accountability

C – Celebrate
T – Take Responsibility
I – I Will
O – Opportunity
N – NOW!

Write them down, find accountability partners that will help you stick to them.

Figure out what makes you happy, find a hobby, make time for you. Doing these things has made a huge improvement in my life. I see things a little clearer now. I have become a little better at controlling my emotions and not allowing everything to just boil up and explode at everyone in my life.

I challenge you, Christian, or not, to take that verse and try to be that Psalm 23 husband.

For me, seeing as I turned my hobby of BJJ into a business, I had to find a new hobby. I friend of mine started a Podcast with me. We talk about life, being a "man", mistakes we have made in life, relationships and how we have messed them up. But we are still pushing forward, growing. When we started it, we came up with the name Hypocrisy 101. We named it that because we are giving advice that we never took, but you should.

Over the past several years I have been told I am strong, and I am inspirational. That I should write a book about everything that I have been through because it might help someone. I still have no clue if writing any of this has helped anyone but me. It really seems like a lot of vomit on paper right now.

I just want people to see, that even when you think your entire life has fallen apart you have to get focused and keep moving forward. Taking your life is not the way to go. Sitting in your own misery does not help either. Relationships can be restored. Divorces do not have to be messy, they can be clean and pleasant. Do not allow your pain to impact those around you. Keep hope alive, focus on the wins no matter how big or small you view them as, focus on them.

That's another thing. As Christians, we say "sin is sin" right? But then we sit here, and we talk about a big blessing and small blessings. How about a mind shift, let's stop categorizing things this way? If sin is sin, then we are miracles, not miracles, why are blessing not blessing, regardless of the impact they have on your life? Sorry, just a little mindset change I have started to implement in my life. People are people, good is good, bad is bad. This has helped me to keep my emotions under control, it has helped me focus on a lot of things and cleared my head. I no longer feel the need to keep value on things like that. I just remain thankful and grateful for the things and people God has blessed me with.

Sing, dance, jump around, laugh. One thing that I do is a will blast music and jump around singing and dancing with my little dude. He laughs so much. and so do I. Some nights he will tell me to dance with him, so I drop what I am doing to turn the song he wants on and start dancing and singing to him. He says most of the words wrong, but we don't care. We are just living our best life and having fun in the moment. Even if I have to listen to the same song a million times, even if I am tired and need sleep. Nothing else matters when he and I are dancing and singing songs.

I am still working on moving forward in life, working on growing into the man God needs me to be. I recognize that I am broken and that without God in my life I am lost.

For you, it could be the universe, or Buda, or whatever. To me it does not matter, if you are not hurting others and growing into the best version of you possible, I am with you on that journey.

Heavenly Father, I pray to you right now. I want You to know how grateful I am for everything that You have blessed me, even the free will to mess things up beyond anything a human can fix. But nothing is so broken that you cannot fix it. Dad, I have spent so many years hating myself and ready to die. But like my friend Travis challenged me to do. I pray to you right now asking you to help me want to live. Dad, I want to live. I want to live a long life. I am ready to come home when You are ready for me. Until that day comes, I want to want to live. Help me to be good with Your will Dad. Your will not mine. You know my heart's desires. You know where I am lacking. Help me to change into the father You want and need me to be. Help me to change into the man You want and need me to be. Help me show Your love and grace. I know I will fail at

*times but help me to forgive myself the way
that You forgive me. Dad, I want to live.*

In Jesus Holy name I pray. Amen

Chapter 24

<u>One Step at a Time</u>

I t is January 17, 2020. A new year and a new me is coming. A year of finally working on finding me, who I am, and who God sees me as. I am not that fucking special or important, I know that. I am just an average guy who had spent his entire life trying to be something I am not. Trying to make others happy, trying to be perfect… whatever, for people. In this messed journey I have done nothing but become selfish, resentful, and just a downright fake and ugly person. I become a monster that just wanted to bleed others dry of their love and self.

Today I make a stand for myself and my family to stop being this way. I will not take other people's issues and problems in an attempt to have people like me or to feed my ego. No more pity parties for me. God is doing a great work in me now. I know he is helping me to change into a better person. I more attentive, kind, and loving person than I have ever been, I still mess up, but I am no longer trying to seek attention. I am someone that can be trusted, someone that can be there for people in a healthy way. One that can set boundaries and not bleed myself out of energy and patience. I can say "no" now. I am not an abusive monster. I have learned to take things one step at a time. The road ahead of me is a rough road. Rewiring my brain to think differently, and to react differently. 41 years of bad habits and emotional damage that I must clean up and rebuild into something better, stronger, loving, and safe.

I finally started to build a solid relationship with God. Learning to lean on Him more every day. I have a lot of great things going on in my life now, not that it is perfect, I am still working on getting healthy, rebuilding my relationship with my oldest son, and my daughter. Keeping my relationship with my little dude strong.

Without God, in my life, I have no clue where I would be right now. Most likely in a ditch or six feet under by now to be honest. I can say that I would not be where I am at for sure.

I have learned that every horrible thing I did to people in the past has had a ripple effect. Like throwing a stone in a pound. At the same time, every good thing I have done has the same impactful ripple effect. I must make the choice every day to make better choices so that the impactful ripples I make in this world are positive and good.

I must set boundaries with people in my life. Healthy ones, for everyone involved. I have spent most of my life enabling people. Not only is this not fair to me, but it is not fair to them either. I do not need to rescue people from their issues, sin, or consequences. If I always do that, I am robbing them of the lessons they need to learn as well as creating codependency which is not healthy either. I have learned that I have tried to rescue people because I feared losing the relationship with that person. I then smothered them, built-up resentment of that person because I never received anything from them that in my mind equaled what I did for them. Which in turn ruined the relationship. Something I tried to stop from happening in the first place. My desire for others superseded my desire for God, meaning I turned all the relationships into idols.

I will no longer be a doormat. Now I am not saying I will be a jerk to people. But by setting healthy boundaries with others I can ensure that I am no longer "bleeding" myself out anymore. To do this I must first figure out my won self-worth. This is an area I have a lot of trouble working through, but I am worth the effort to figure it out. My children are worth it too, my future is worth it, and most importantly my mental health and life are worth the effort.

It is ok to help people, and sometimes the best way to do that is to allow them to take care of the issue themselves, and just be there alongside them. I don't have to take the issue and try to fix it myself.

Still working on being a better communicator. The Bible tells us that we have the power to speak death and life. As you can see, I have spoken a lot of death into my life and relationships. Thus, why I am in the position I am in. I was never good at listening to what people were telling me, I just jumped to conclusions and started trying to "fix" the problem. Emotionally driven void of any and all logic. That caused me to speak emotionally instead of logically, which hurt the people closest to me and put distance between us. No longer will I uses phrases like "do you want me to slit my wrists and bleed myself dry?" or "I'm done..." No, these phrases hold people hostage emotionally. They are not fair to them. I am learning to take more of a structured time out. It's ok to tell someone that you need time to think about a topic and to ask for time to think it over. Let them know when you can come back to this topic to discuss it. Then follow through with it. Don't procrastinate.

Forgiving myself has got to be the most difficult thing I have ever tried to do. Looking back at my life and seeing what I have done to the people closest to me than trying to forgive myself just seems overwhelming and impossible at times. But I am no longer quitting on myself or my family. This is something we all must do in our life, forgive. Forgive those who have hurt us and forgive ourselves for hurting others. This is a process for sure.

Make a battel plan for all of this. Build that road map so that you can follow it step by step. Stick to it every day. You are going to have bad days but remember that if you mess up, it's ok. There is always tomorrow too, the next hour, and the next minute to reset and get back on track with your plan.

I wish I could tell you all that this was a great epiphany that I had, and that this was all my idea. It was not. These are all things that I learned from my Life Coach, Amy Hill, and I am sure you could just find all this info online. So, like me, go find your Amy. Find help now, don't wait till it is "too late". Not that it is ever too late. With God in your life, all things are possible. Learn to live by His will.

Even if you don't believe in Christ, there are so many amazing guidelines and principles of life to follow in the Bible that we can all follow, and I believe that if we did, this world would be a much better please, suicide rates would be lower, divorce rates would be lower. People would be happier and more successful. Again, the world would be a much better place if we were all kind and loving to each other.

I would like to pray for you, the reader if that is ok with you.

> *Heavenly Father, I come to you right now*
> *with a humble, yet heavy heart. Dad in this*
> *world You created there is so much pain.*
> *People killing themselves over being bullied,*
> *men taking their lives due to divorce. I am*
> *one of those who has been hurt by both*
> *being bullied and two divorces. I thank You*
> *for being with me every step of the way, and*
> *not allowing the enemy to win. I thank You*
> *for every breath, every day, and every*
> *opportunity You have presented me with. I*
> *pray that You help the readers of this book to*
> *see that they are loved, they are worth it,*
> *and that You can help them. You can fix the*
> *issues they are dealing with. Help them to*
> *connect with You on a whole new level, as*
> *You have me. Show them Your love and*

grace. Forgive us all and help us to learn how to forgive ourselves. Help us draw closer to You every day. Help us see ourselves the way You see us, perfect and loved. We just want to enjoy the lives you have blessed us with, enjoy it alongside the people you have connected with us.

I pray for any relationship that is currently being attacked by the enemy, help the men and women reading this. Help them to connect with each other on a whole new level, one that cannot be touched by the enemy.

Protect us, Your children, from the enemy who seeks to kill, steal, and destroy. Bless our futures Dad.

In Jesus Holy name I pray, Amen!

I hope that after reading all the drama and self-pity in my life, it has helped you in some way. Maybe, maybe not, but I thank you for following me on this little journey of my past.

Now go out there and claim your victories, dance life away, pray, meditate, relax. Find you, love you, love life. Make your life story an amazing thing. Don't wait any longer to ask or seek help. Every day we have to fight, it is a battle, a war. So, let's step in the cage together. Brush that dust off, get your bearings, ring that fucking bell. I have a lot more rounds left and so do you. We are all fighters, we are not quitters. It's time to take a deep breath, now let it out slowly. Focus on what it is you want. What are you going to do to get it? Ding, ding. Let's do this shit.

Chapter 25

Sayings, Quotes, Scripture

Here we are, almost done. I just wanted to add one last chapter for everyone. It should be kind of quick, heck maybe you can even skip it now and come back a little later. I just thought I would share a few sayings, quotes, scriptures, and songs that helped me get through the past few years, months, weeks, days, hours, and minutes. Some may seem strange but remember who is writing this all out. I will do my best to give credit where it is due here. I listen to a lot of sleep meditation videos and words of affirmation videos on YouTube as well, just search for them you will find plenty out there.

When you are feeling down and out, but something great just happened, recognize it with a simple little phrase like

"Boom!" – Al Tito Delara

"Solid!" – Well, that's mine.

Come up with your own, trust me you might feel stupid saying it out loud to yourself, but it helps.

Quotes:

"It is perfectly okay to admit you're not okay." – No clue just saw it on social media.

"Be humble and never think you are better than anyone else. "For dust you are and dust you shall return". – Again, saw this one on social media.

"Train tirelessly to defeat the greatest enemy, yourself, and to discover the greatest master, yourself." – Shi Su Yan

"Don't miss something that could be great just because it could be difficult."

"The devil makes sin comfortable. He fills our cells with everything we think we want, yet he leaves the door open. Outside that door is scary, difficult, and painful looking. Like a huge thorn bush. Why? Because Jesus is on the other side of that thorn bush, and the enemy doesn't want us going to Him." – Brianna Nicole Miller

"Remember that you want the changes that you are making to be permanent and lasting... like the butterfly... a whole new you! Not a transformer that will change back and forth." – Amy Hill

"You must tell yourself, "No matter how hard it is, or how hard it gets, I'm going to make it." – Les Brown

"The irony is that while God Doesn't need us but still wants us, we desperately need God but don't want him most of the time." – Francis Chan

"Never be a prisoner of your past. It was just a lesson, not a life sentence." – Another social media post.

"I love you, daddy, you are amazing and strong. I just wish you could see it." – Sydney Bowers AKA Baby Girl

"You have to learn to become comfortable in uncomfortable situations." – Coach Robert Peters

Scripture:

Genesis 2:21-22

Psalm 147:3

Joshua 1:9

John 16:33

Psalm 23

Ephesians 5:25

Ruth 1:16-17

Mathew 7:24-25

Exodus 14:14

Isaiah 60:22

Sure, I could come up with a lot more, but these right here have made a huge impact on my life, and I hope something here helps you too.

Epilogue

Have you ever been in a situation that looks hopeless? Like there is no way out of the problem or situation? Like there is no way you can ever love again, or be loved again? Ever feel like all you do is fuck things up over, and over again? Have you given up on everything and just decided that this is how your life will always be? Just giving up on hope. Well, you are not alone, as you can see that is my entire life. All but that last part. I have not given up on hope.

I could go all Christian on you guys here, but I want to be a little different here. For those of you who don't believe, I want you to know that there are plenty of people out there going through the same things as you. There are people out there, in your life, who love you deeply. These people care about you so much. They want the best for you as well.

Don't allow your emotions to take control of you in a negative way. Don't allow them to take you to the darkest places. Understand that you are important and have a purpose in life. Whatever is going on in your life, it is not too late. It is never too late.

If it is a pending divorce or a breakup and you don't want to have that happen, start making the changes you need right now. Stop waiting for others to take care of the problems for you. Seek help now. As a Christ-follower, I seek God for my help. He then presents people or guides me to people, who can and will help. At the same time, he presents me with the solutions. All I have to do is pay attention, listen, hear Him, and take the next step.

I believe that He does the same for people who don't believe in Him. Just listen, open your eyes and ears in your dark moments. When you hear that little whisper, that loving and kind whisper. The one that causes zero confusion. That is the voice the listen to.

Remember that it is not alright to put your damage on other people as I did. Take ownership of your actions,

To the men reading this.

If your marriage seems like it's going towards divorce, I say this to you. Pull your head out of your ass. We don't have all the answers. It is ok to talk about your emotions, just don't let them take over. Talk to your wife in a kind loving way, listen to her and see what the issue is. Ask questions, don't assume. If the conversation is going nowhere, take a "time out". Don't walk away, slam doors, punch walls.

Don't present her with the solutions you think are correct. Work with her on a solution. Allow her to give input. Make sure she feels like you value her opinion. Make sure she feels like an equal to you, because that is exactly what she is your equal. You are not above her. It is perfectly fine to admit you need help, it is not a weakness. On the contrary, that is what being a strong man looks like. That does not give you a license to dump every issue on her.

To the ladies.

Remember this, please. We may act strong and like we have everything under control, but a lot of the time we need your help. Your input, guidance, and ideas are always needed and wanted. At the same time the advice I just gave to men, please take that all into consideration as well.

Marriage is a partnership, "it takes two to tango". Men have emotions too, and they are valid and should not be brushed off as him "not being a man".

We need to learn how to be comfortable in uncomfortable situations. We need to learn to become better communicators with people. I hope that some of what I have shared shows, people, at least what not to do in life, and relationships. I hope that you can see what life looks like when you are emotionally, verbally, and mentally abusive to people, you will end up with a very lonely person as I have become. If you are already in my shoes? Well again, there is hope. Keep working on becoming the best version of you possible. Keep growing.

You don't want to wait to make these needed changes. You might miss out on some important life events as a parent like I am currently missing out on. It will hurt more than you think. Need another example? Here you go. My baby girl is currently shopping for a prom dress. Something I always pictured being a part of. Seeing her in every beautiful dress and seeing her smile light up when she finds the perfect dress. Not this dad. All the damage I caused in life, has caused her to not include me in that experience.

If I cannot what more will I miss out on? Engagements, weddings, grandkids? I don't know and don't want to know. I want to change so I don't miss out on anymore.

Are you still wondering what the point of this book is? Welcome to the club. I will say this, whatever this book spoke into your life, whatever it means to you, well then, that was the point of it.

Remember this though… *"We must learn to become comfortable in uncomfortable situations"*. Once we can do this, I truly believe that we can make it through anything in life.

Acknowledgments

I know my writing style is not that great, I never was good at writing things. I mean let's be real, it sucks, I think my three-year-old could write better than me. I was never good writing papers in school, professional emails, or personally. You know like love notes and birthday cards. I have to give create to this entire book to God first. You never gave up on me, You have not forsaken me, You love me.

I want to give thanks to my Life Coach Amy Hill, for her program and all the time and effort she put into creating it. Without her program, I would not have figured out how to start making the changes I needed in my life. I would not have been able to start working on loving myself. I would have remained the monster I was and continued to destroy everything in my path. Your program might be called *"The Powerful Marriage"* but it is about so much more than a marriage.

I gotta thank my kids. All the insight they have given me, the recognition of some of the changes they see in me. The real talks about what kind of person I was. Thank you three for loving me through my bad times. Thank you for believing in me. I promise dad is going to get better, and things will be better for us.

Thank you to all my friends who have stuck with me through all my pity parties and issues. Thank you for checking up on me and making sure I am ok.

Thank you, Al, for listening to my pity parties, for kicking me in the ass and talking real with me. Thank you for the challenges that helped me focus more on God than the devastation going on in my life.

I want to thank Bri. You stepped up and became a mother to my older two kids, you did not have to do that, but you did out of unconditional love for me and them. Our eight years together sure had their struggles, but there were plenty of amazing times too. You supported me starting this book years ago. Even after our divorce, you have still done things that most ex-wives don't do for their ex-husbands. Still caring for the older two kids and loving them like they were your own. You will always have a special place in my heart regardless of where we go from here. I would not blame you for hating me for all the damage I caused you and your family. But you don't for some reason. Thank you for showing me what true love really is, and for helping me find Jesus.

CPSIA information can be obtained
at www.ICGtesting.com
Printed in the USA
LVHW030718260420
654459LV00003B/369